Foxfield　　　　Sow How　　Pool Garth　　　　Gummers How

Swallowmire　　St. Anthony's Church　　Hodge Hill　　Chapel House　　Bridge House

LIFE ON THE FELL

A Pictorial Chronicle of a Lakeland Community

HELEN CALDWELL   JENNIFER FORSYTH
JOHN CALDWELL   BERYL OFFLEY

on behalf of
The Cartmel Fell and District Local History Society

Cover Photograph:
Fred Cockerton, Rowland and Billy Long at "The Office",
Pool Garth, Cartmel Fell, c. 1890

Rear Cover Photograph:
Winter on Ludderburn Hill

Copyright ©2000 All rights reserved. No part of this book may be reproduced or transmitted in any form or by any means, electronic or mechanical, including photocopy, without permission in writing from the authors. Reviewers may quote brief passages.

First published in November 2000
by
Curlew Productions
Thirlestane House
Kelso TD5 8PD
Scotland

First Edition printed November 2000, reprinted March 2001

ISBN 1 900259 96 6

Design and layout: Curlew Productions, Kelso TD5 8PD
Maps drawn by John Offley
Set in Optima 10.6/12

Printed by Kelso Graphics, Kelso TD5 7BH, Scotland

CONTENTS

1. SCHOOLDAYS	*1*
2. WORKING LIFE	*16*
3. WORSHIP	*38*
4. SOCIAL LIFE	*50*
5. FAMILIES OF NOTE	*70*
The Birket Family of Cartmel Fell	70
The Poole Family of Cartmel Fell	75
The Walker Family of Bowland Bridge	77
The Matthews Family	81
The Taylors of Thorphinsty Hall	86
The Batty Family	91
6. FAMOUS PEOPLE	*94*
The Barbers of Bowland Bridge	94
William Gibson 1720 - 1791	96
William Pearson of Borderside 1780 - 1856	98
The Simpsons at Gill Head	101
Arthur Ransome at Ludderburn	104
Sir John Fisher of Blakeholme Wray	106
7. UNUSUAL EVENTS	*108*
Royal Visits	108
Lake Winster	110
Rebuilding Bowland Bridge	116
INDEX	*121*
Suggested Reading	126

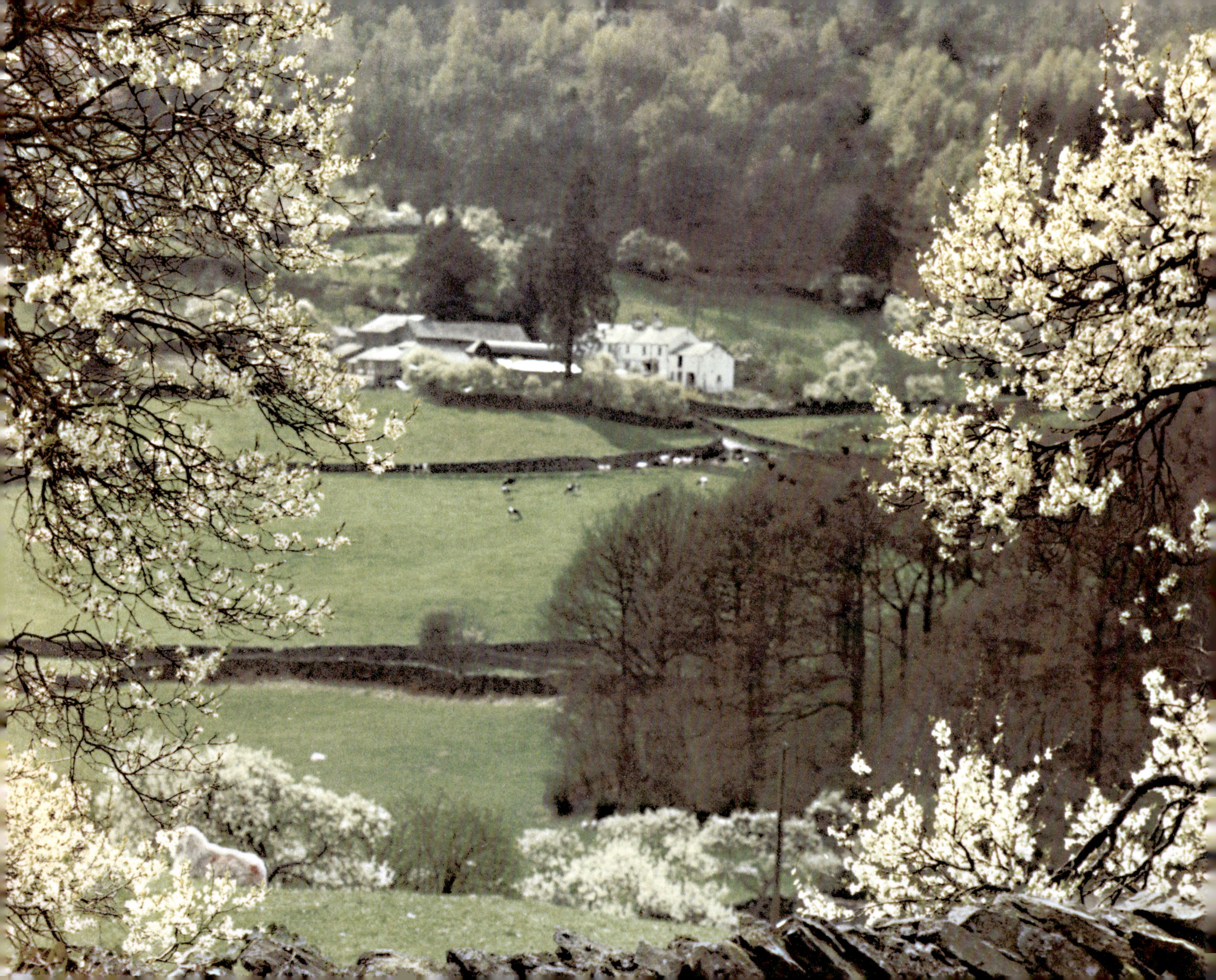

FOREWORD

This book had its origins about 25 years ago, when the late David Caldwell, aided and abetted by Bill Adam, began to collect old photographs of local people, places and events. Many of these came from family collections and snapshot albums, and were in varying states of preservation; but David and his wife Helen were able to use their photographic skills to copy them.

After David died in 1985, Bill Adam took charge of the album of photographs and, as it was passed around local families, more photographs were collected and more names added to the captions. When in 1993, the Cartmel Fell and District Local History Society (CFDLHS) was established under the leadership of Jennifer Forsyth, it was agreed that the new Society should become the custodian of the growing collection of photographs and other records. The task of accurately identifying the dates, events and personalities portrayed, and of indexing and preserving them for posterity, involved much effort, especially by Beryl Offley, and there are now more than 300 pictures in this remarkable social record.

Since its foundation, the History Society has also encouraged its members towards research – through local archives and records, folk-lore, visits and other enquiries – into many aspects of the history of this rural community. So that, when considering ways by which the new millennium might be marked, a proposal was made to produce a book which would combine a selection of the best photographs with some commentary based on local history research; and this found widespread support.

The resulting "Life on the Fell" does not purport to be a detailed historical account of life through the centuries in this corner of Cumbria; but it is offered more as a "pictorial chronicle", which may revive memories of bygone days, and preserve images of times past. It may also show that although much has changed in rural life, there continues to be a strong sense of community within the scattered population of our parishes. The availability of photographs has of course limited the visual record of social and working lives to within the past 150 years; but in other chapters – on Worship, on local Families and Famous People – research among the archives and domestic records has provided a longer perspective, over four or more centuries.

The final compilation has resulted mainly from the shared work of four members of CFDLHS. Jennifer Forsyth wrote the first draft of most of the text; Helen Caldwell used computer techniques to maximise the quality of the photographs and to produce family trees; while Beryl Offley (whose husband John prepared the maps) and John Caldwell undertook various other editorial tasks. Although much effort has been devoted to checking historical facts and figures, the vagaries of memory and the uncertainties of oral history mean that there may well be mistakes or disputes over detail. The editorial team willingly shoulders any blame; because for them this recording and celebration of Life on the Fell has really been of a labour of love.

*Opposite:
Great Hartbarrow seen from Barkbooth in damson blossom time.*

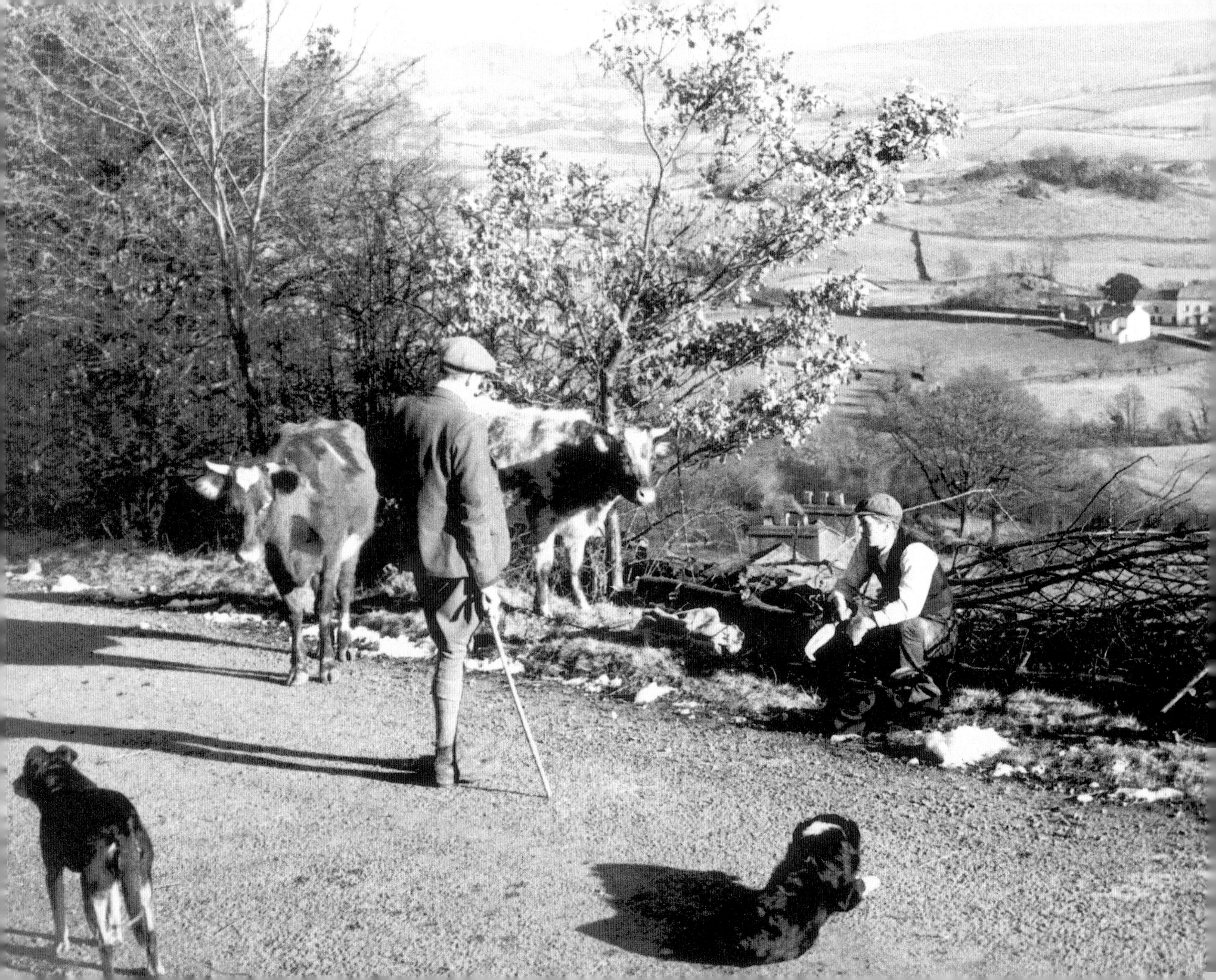

ACKNOWLEDGEMENTS

A book of old photographs and memories of a widespread community must inevitably draw deeply on the contributions of many people. The help of all those who have assisted this project in a variety of ways is warmly acknowledged. To any who have inadvertently been omitted from the following list, both apologies and gratitude are offered:

Bill Adam, Jackie Bailey, Michael Berry,
Terry Belshaw, Jean Caldwell,
Josephine Casson, Jonathan Chambers, Elizabeth Cleasby,
Margaret Dawson, John Dench, Joan Duke, Philip Edwards,
Alan Forsyth, John Handley, James Herd,
Eric Kitchen, Bruce Logan, Janet Martin,
Jim and Anne Martindale,
Marjorie and William Matthews,
Dorothy Newton, Michael Newton,
John Offley, Leslie Park, Nicola Pattison,
John and Ivy Pearson, Mary Phizacklea,
Jean Simpson, David Smail, Audrey Smith,
Paul and Sylvia Stewart, Connie Thistlethwaite, Geoff Wightman,
Ella Wilkinson, Lucy Wooff, and James Wright.

Thanks are due also to all those, if not named above, who have provided photographs for the Cartmel Fell and District Local History Society collection; and the help of the Margaret Duff Collection is much appreciated. We are also conscious of the debt we owe to many long-departed photographers, such as Richard Cragghill, whose skills ensured such vivid pictures of life and times many decades ago. For all the illustrations used, we have used our best endeavours to establish any copyright ownership, and these too are acknowledged. If any other person feels they may have a legitimate claim of this kind, we should be pleased to hear from them.

Opposite: Bowland Bridge from Strawberry Bank, c. 1940

We wish also to record our sincere thanks to those organisations and individuals who have provided financial support towards the production of this book. We gratefully acknowledge the assistance of:

– The Local Heritage Initiative, which is a partnership between the Heritage Lottery Fund, Nationwide Building Society and the Countryside Agency;

– Cumbria County Council, through their Grange, Cartmel and Lyth Valley Neighbourhood Forum;

– South Lakeland District Council, through their Millennium Grant Programme;

– The Kirby Archives Trust;

– The Cartmel Fell and District Local History Society.

The advice and support of Jim Grisenthwaite, Barry Mackay and Michael Smith in connection with fund-raising for this project were also greatly appreciated.

The Editors

Cartmel Fell

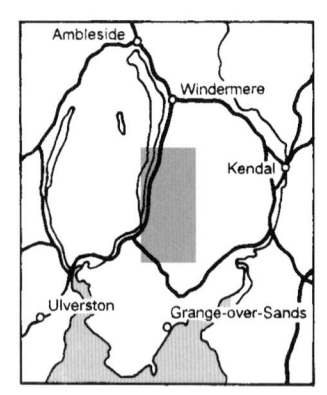

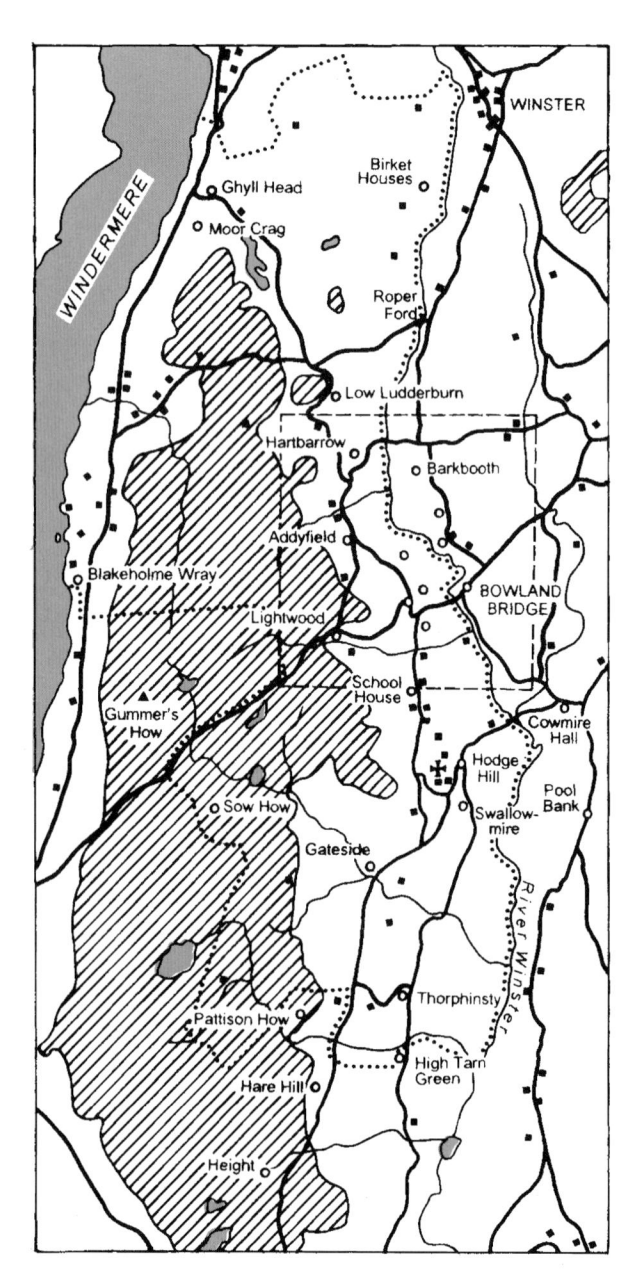

CARTMEL FELL AND THE WINSTER VALLEY

- ○ Places/dwellings featured in photographs
- ■ Other dwellings
- ✠ St. Anthony's Church
- .... Parish Boundary
- ▨ Land over 150 metres

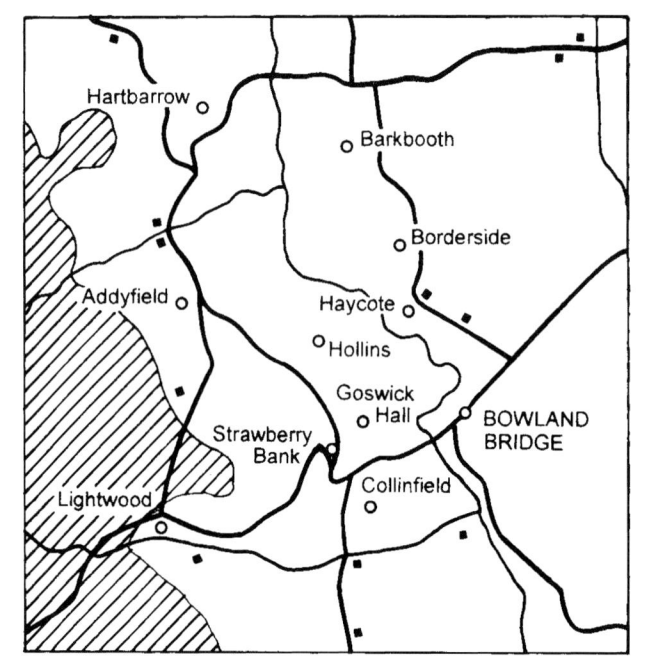

x

INTRODUCTION

As one approaches the Lake District from the south, Morecambe Bay is first glimpsed against a backdrop of the South Lakeland fells – the limestone ridges of Scout Scar and Whitbarrow, and, further west, Cartmel and Newton Fells running south to the bay at Grange-over-Sands. Between Whitbarrow and Cartmel Fell lies the Winster Valley, where the river, over much of its length from Winster village down to Lindale, formerly divided Westmorland from Lancashire-North-of-the-Sands. The map opposite shows that the parish of Cartmel Fell is about six miles long and three to four miles wide, with the long north-south axis being a ridge which rises in places to around 700 feet.

Cartmel Fell and the Winster Valley north and south of Bowland Bridge provide the setting for this book. Although located at the doorstep of the more mountainous Lake District, loved and visited by so many, this is a part of South Lakeland known to fewer people. Away from the main arteries of traffic to the tourist centres, our area is a haven of relative quiet, a delightful confusion of narrow winding lanes, and sudden steep climbs up on to the Fell, where the ridge, topped by Gummers How, offers ever-changing views to every quarter. It is an area, too, which enjoys an equable climate, with more sun and less rain than in the mountains to the north. Harsh winters are rare, though the occasional memorable snowfall – as in the winter of 1995/6 – can bring a different kind of beauty to the landscape.

This has always been a rather isolated, and thereby self-contained, neighbourhood. For centuries before enclosure and systematic drainage, it was difficult of access, as both the Lyth and Winster Valleys were little more than marshy northward extensions of Morecambe Bay. Even the first roads west from Kendal required such treacherous ascents of Cartmel Fell, via Tow Top or Strawberry Bank, that the hazardous route to Furness across the sands of the Bay was often preferred to the rough and muddy inland tracks.

But the very remoteness of the Fell had its attractions too, not least for those such as religious dissenters (see Chapter 3) seeking freedom from officialdom; and the "hard land" above the marshy valley bottoms with their plentiful peat reserves, offered opportunities for farming. The place names and farmsteads betray their Norse origins in the Thwaites, Hows and Fells; but the "land of Cartmel" had been settled much earlier, in St. Cuthbert's time, and the Romans would have been provisioned by local farmers. So the clearance of farm land must have been a long, slow process.

The walls which can now be seen marching up precipitous fellsides are only about 200 years old, a result of successive Enclosure Acts, and the now dense and towering woodlands would have been less than half the height during the seventeenth and eighteenth centuries, because coppicing then took place every fifteen years or so.

Cartmel Fell

The Great Snowfall - February 1996 – on Thorphinsty Hill

Most of the farm houses now considered as old were built or rebuilt in the 17th century, a result of the end of Border warfare when James the sixth of Scotland and first of England united the two kingdoms, to begin a period of growing agricultural prosperity. One can sometimes see traces of an older building embedded in Jacobean work, and a few pele towers remain, such as at Cowmire Hall – reminders of the days of terrible Scottish raids.

Tenure of land in these northern border counties was different from the southern feudal system, because here a mobile force was needed for defence. Yeomen held their land in perpetuity in return for border service, but paid an annual fine to the Lord of their manor, and also at the death of either the Lord or the owner. This independence produced a race of farmers who lived by co-operating on large tasks and who could make their own decisions as to farming policy.

Today in Cartmel Fell there is still no village or large cluster of dwellings, and the ancient farmsteads are scattered at regular intervals over the landscape, like flowers on a print dress. The panorama of Fell and Valley is perhaps best seen from the western escarpment of Whitbarrow (see inside covers), and at first glance suggests a very thinly populated countryside. But a discerning eye can from there pick out nearly all the farms and notable houses, the two inns, St. Anthony's church, and most of the other places featured in this book. From there too, one can visualise the awful consequences of a proposal made nearly 40 years ago (see Chapter 7), whereby the beautiful patchwork of fields and farms in the valley below would have disappeared forever beneath 50 feet of water.

It is not very long ago that people might have spent their entire lives in this secluded neighbourhood of 30 or 40 square miles of fell and valley. Certainly, as Chapter 5 shows, there have been many generations of the same families hereabouts for two or three centuries. The pictures recapture something of the lives they led - childhood days at the little fellside school (Chapter 1); worship at the nearby church (Chapter 3); the working days dominated by seasonal tasks in farm and woodland (Chapter 2); and the

The Great Snowfall of February 1996 – the Winster Valley from High Tarn Green.

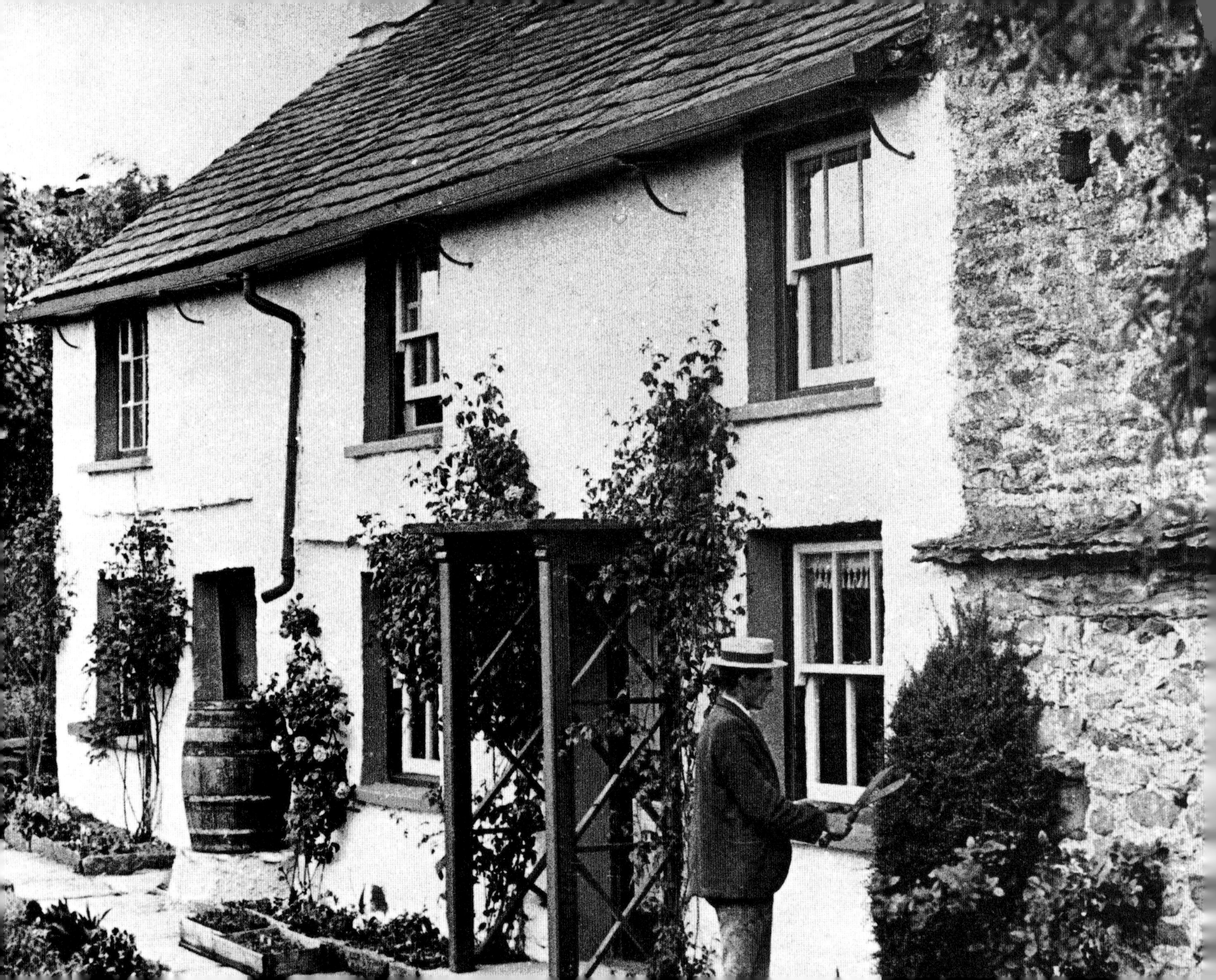

Robert James Watson mowing near Hartbarrow.

Opposite: Lightwood Cottage in the 1920s.

variety of social and sporting entertainment they enjoyed then and now (Chapter 4). Just occasionally there have emerged from humble beginnings individuals who went on to achieve distinction in the wider world (Chapter 6); and, in a similarly random way, a few unusual events (Chapter 7) have occurred which disturbed or enlivened the tranquillity of life on the fell.

Such is the pictorial chronicle presented in the following pages. No doubt every rural community has its own historical tapestry of people, places and happenings. But to those who have known Cartmel Fell and the Winster Valley – and perhaps for those who might come to know this Cumbrian corner through the pages of this book – it will always be a unique and special place.

Stan Mattinson leading the Coniston pack over Bowland Bridge

1. SCHOOLDAYS

The Schoolmaster - Pastor

It is known that in many rural communities the church or chapel was the original schoolroom, no other being available. The persons most qualified to teach were the curate or "reader", and they performed the dual role of schoolmaster and pastor, working six days a week. The former would have had some university education, and the latter would have attended the local Grammar school at least.

The remoter areas of the Lake District were not attractive to ordained clergymen, as the stipends were so small in the 17th and 18th centuries, though later improved by Queen Anne's Bounty. To help maintain a church-going population, a class of readers was created, and they did just that, i.e. read the lessons and prayers; but they were not allowed to preach sermons as they had not been ordained.

The curates and readers were usually as poor as, or poorer than, members of the community they served, so some additional income was essential, and this was frequently earned by teaching. Many clergymen were small farmers; and one of the best known was "Wonderful Walker", who taught the children in the church at Seathwaite, in the Duddon valley, whilst spinning his own wool. Wordsworth left us a description of this rural pastor:

"His seat was within the rails of the altar; the communion table was his desk, and, like Shenstone's schoolmistress, the master employed himself at the

1. The first school group photograph, taken in 1872 when this school building had just opened. Revd. William Summers is on the right.

Modern maps still mark a School near St. Anthony's church on the wooded eastern slopes of Cartmel Fell above Hodge Hill; but, like so many other rural parishes, this has lost its school, which now serves as the Parish Hall. The building is a relatively recent structure, with a datestone of 1872.

This building, and the original school which had been nearby, demonstrates the determination of the parish to give their children an education; and to that end they had struggled for centuries.

Cartmel Fell

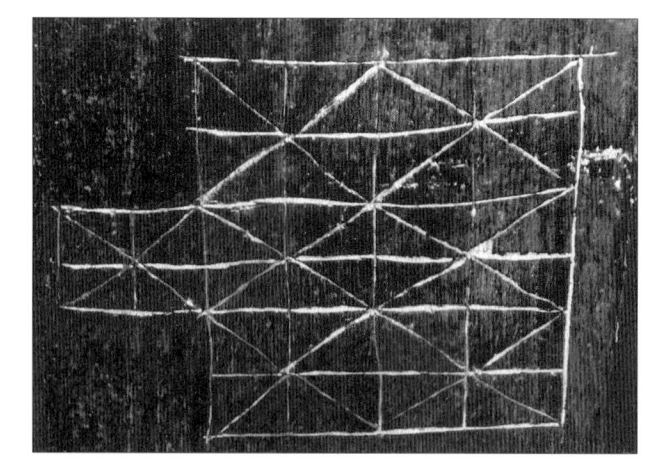

2. The incised grid patterns inside the Cowmire Hall pew in the church.

spinning wheel, while the children were repeating their lessons at his side."

Some evidence of this intimate association of the church with teaching can be seen in St. Anthony's church on Cartmel Fell. On the benches inside the Cowmire Hall pew are some incised grid patterns, which may have been the means of teaching fractions or multiplication, perhaps using a system devised by John Napier (1550-1617).

This pew is of the box variety, and a table is fixed in the centre where six or eight children might sit. Around the sides of the pew are bench seats which would accommodate perhaps a dozen more.

Head - hunting for Teachers

In 1695, Benjamin Fletcher left £200 in his will, to be invested, the interest from which was to be used for schoolmasters in Lindale, Flookburgh, Staveley and Cartmel Fell. Even if the interest was as high as 5%, the four schoolmasters would receive only £2 10s. each per year, so one gets an idea of the lowly status of the teacher.

We know quite a lot about the difficulties of maintaining a school in Cartmel Fell from the diaries and letters of the Brockbank family[1]. Two years after Benjamin Fletcher's bequest came into being, Thomas Brockbank wrote that he thought the schoolmaster at Cartmel Fell lacked diligence and care. He had heard that William Myles of Blawith had a good reputation and suggested Mr. Myles as a replacement. Head-hunting is not a recent phenomenon.

By 1700, however, Myles too was out of favour with the vicar of Cartmel, and he was dismissed. There seems to have been a good deal of personal enmity between the two men, and Myles complained to the Bishop of Chester that he had not been paid the promised augmented salary. This was probably Benjamin Fletcher's £2 10s.. Thomas Brockbank commented wryly:

"Admittedly, the people of Cartmel Fell were Factious and Headdy, yet they had too just cause for complaint."

Some diplomatic moves must have ensued, as the Bishop of Chester withdrew his injunction on Myles; but from the letters of Thomas Brockbank we know that by 1706, Jonah Walker was the appointed reader and schoolmaster at Cartmel Fell. By that time, the previous vicar of Cartmel, Thomas Proddy, had become senile[2] and had been succeeded by none other than Thomas Brockbank.

Thomas Brockbank's Problems

Upon stepping into office, Thomas immediately set about making enquiries as to Jonah Walker's whereabouts. It seems that the schoolmaster was missing from his post, and indeed had not taught at the school for two years. While Thomas Proddy was still nominally the vicar of Cartmel, Thomas Brockbank had not the authority to pursue matters, but he must have been aware of the discontent in Cartmel Fell. Copious letters flew from his pen after the missing reader's brother suggested that Queen's College, Oxford might be a good place to start enquiries. It transpired that Mr. Walker had abandoned his flock to better himself, and without informing his vicar or his parishioners, had decided to take a degree and thus improve his salary. The parish was in uproar, declaring that: *"They had been left in a manner Desolate ever since."*

The absence of a preacher and teacher was a serious matter to the Church of England at that period of history, as it left the camp unguarded. The upsurge of dissenters, non-conformists and Catholics since the Act of Toleration in 1689 was a real threat to the stability of the parish. Quakers abounded, and a non-conformist academy had been set up at Hartbarrow in 1684, having moved there from Dawson Fold in the Lyth valley.

Bryan Philipson of Hodge Hill, who was probably the equivalent of a school governor, received a copy of the letter that Thomas Brockbank had written to Jonah Walker's tutor at Oxford. Philipson replied with ill-concealed exasperation:

"Sir, Having perused yr. letters, I am glad that you have heard from Mr. Walker, and also from his Tutor and when he intends to come down. If you had not written up, we sho'd never had one line of him; either where he was or of his return."

There was more in the same vein of furious criticism, but the letter ended with an urgent plea:

"Ye winter season is coming on, for having any schole it is best to see you in ye event thereof."

Reading between the lines, it would seem that schooling was impractical in the worst of winter months. The church could not be heated, and the farms were so isolated, the roads being almost non-existent. From further correspondence of Thomas Brockbank's, we learn that Mr. Walker never did return to Cartmel Fell, but took a curacy in the West Country for £25 per annum; but he did not have the courage or the courtesy to tell Thomas Brockbank.

During this tiresome period, a Mr. Hotblack had been engaged to read prayers on some Sundays, but when the situation became clear, his position was regularised, and he was in the position of reader and schoolmaster until 1710.

Difficult Years - 1710 to 1870

This irregular and patchy scholastic course continued, and one suspects that only the most determined children could have made much progress. In a memorandum of 1726, referred to in an HMSO pamphlet in 1900[3], the trend is in the same pattern:

Cartmel Fell

"Whereas such small encouriagement hath for severall years by past for keeping a constant school in Cartmelfell, to the detriment of the children thereof, whose parents would constantly send them to school; Wee, whose names are hereunto subscribed, neighbours and inhabitants in the chapelry of Cartmell-fell, being verry sensible of the loss occasioned thereby, Do hereby give our severall consents to take up and appropriate the graseing and eatage of a piece of comon, already and time out of mind almost enclosed and called the Stock Moss, (the income) for the sole use of a teaching schoolmaster."

The income from the moss in 1900 was £9 10s. a year, with an extra £2 8s. for the shooting rights.

This same pamphlet records the building of the schoolhouse in 1872, but mentions that the old one had been out of use for six years, owing to its dilapidated condition; and that there was nowhere for the schoolmaster to live. We know from descriptions and old maps that the so-called "school" had been on the other side of the road from the present building; and when considered unfit for the children, had been used to house a family of paupers.

3. Mr. Richard Cragghill's first year as teacher, 1896. **Front row,** *second left is Harold Walker. Behind him is Sidney Walker.* **Second row,** *the first girl is Rachel Batty.*

4. School group, with Mr Richard Cragghill, taken about 1903.
Front row:
4 – Dixon Fox (Ashes).
Second row:
*1 – Nellie Batty,
7 & 8 – Florrie & Jonnie Carruthers (Cowmire Hall),
9 & 10 – Fred & Edith Atkinson (Collinfield),
13,14 & 15 - Emily, Alfred & Maggie Birkett (Sow How).*
Back row:
*1 – Mrs. Mary Cragghill,
2 – Caroline Kidd.*

A New School and Schoolmaster – Mr. Cragghill

After the Education Act of 1870 had provided a new framework for primary education for all, the worst of the struggle was over. The log books which the teachers were obliged to keep may be read at the Cumbria Record Office in Barrow. Some are very dull and give no insights into school life, unlike those of Mr. Cragghill, who was headmaster, and at first the only master, for nearly forty years.

He began teaching at Cartmel Fell in January 1896, and he records the weather, the epidemics and great dread of scarlet fever, the nature walks, his pride at his pupils' handling of an HM inspection, and many out-of-school activities. He worried about bird's nesting, and obtained guidance as to conservation from the *Westmorland Gazette*, which published a list of endangered birds, including owls, birds of prey and kingfishers.

Cartmel Fell

Head Teachers at Cartmel Fell School.

1868 - 1875	Isaac Robinson
1875 - 1876	Thomas Chadwick
1877 - 1880	Joseph Waring
1880 - 1893	John White
1893 - 1895	Henry Broadbridge
1896 - 1931	Richard Cragghill
1931 - 1933	Mary Cooper
1933 - 1951	Ruth Glaister
1951 - 1958	Joan Ellison
1958	Mrs. Baines
1958 - 1959	Jean McGowan
1959 - 1971	Caroline Morrison

5 & 6. Two photographs taken in the early 1900's by Mr. Cragghill. The children have been posed at play in front of the school. The first shows the girls v boys in a tug-of-war, and in the second some of the children appear to be playing "Oranges & Lemons" while the boys are engaged in Cumberland and Westmorland Wrestling. The north end of Whitbarrow Scar can be seen in the background.

7. School group taken about 1911.
Front row: *1 – Nancy Matthews, 2 – Mary Taylor (High Tarn Green), 3 – Essie Crowe (Little Thorphinsty), 4 – Nancy Pearson (Borderside), 5 – Florrie Crowe (Little Thorphinsty), 8 – Robin Matthews (Nancy's brother), 13 – Hilton Walker.*
Second row: *1 – Myrtle Lishman, 3 & 4 – John & Margaret Taylor (High Tarn Green), 11 – Agnes Annie Shepherd (Woodside Cottage), 12 – Myles Batty, 14 – Miss Ada Mashiter (teacher).*
Third row: *1 – Maggie Harrison (Foxfield), 2 – Frances Carruthers (Cowmire), 3 – Hilda Taylor (Woodside), 5 – Becky Carruthers (Simpson Ground), 6 – Ernie Shepherd.*
Back row: *3 – Jenny Fletcher (Bryan Beck), 4 – Annie Carruthers (Simpson Ground), 7 – Billy Taylor (High Tarn Green), 9 – Bigland Batty, 10 – Ted Harrison.*

Cartmel Fell

8. Children of all ages were taught in a single class room until 1913, when the second room was constructed.

10. Teacher – Miss Ada Mashiter, probably taken during the Fist World War.

9. Woodwork class 1918. Gate made by Ernie Shepherd, aged 14.

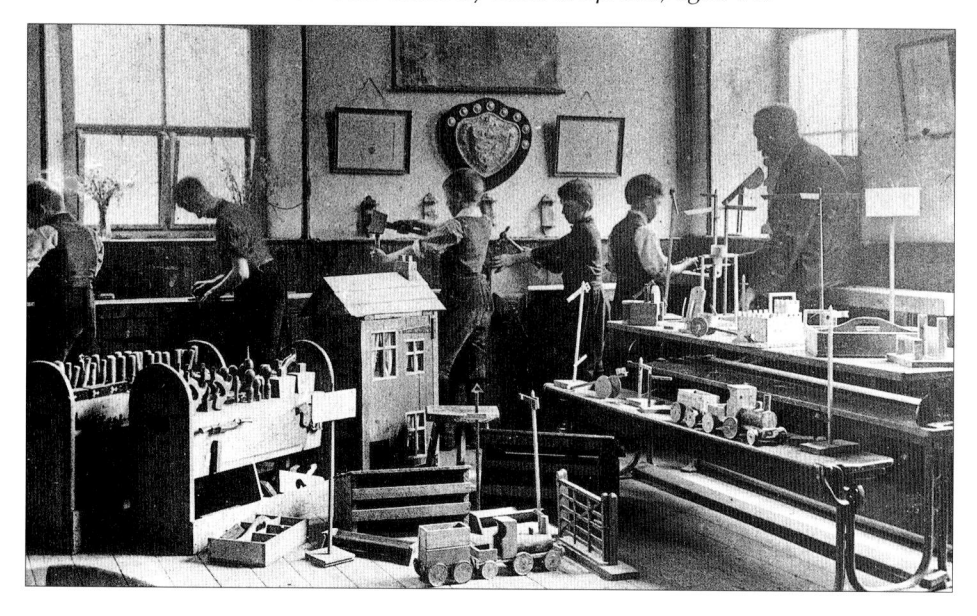

Schooldays

11. School group taken about 1927.
Front row: 1 – Elsie Matthews, 2 – Geoffrey Harrison,
3 – Harold Ellis, 4 – Dick Harrison, 5 – Eddie Long,
6 – Gladys Pearson.
Second row: 1 – Bertha Dixon, 2 – Mary Ellis,
3 – Annie Brockbank, 4 – Mary Kellett,
5 – Eileen Kellett, 6 – Margaret Fleming,
7 – Cathy Thornbarrow.
Third row: 1 – Sally Fleming, 2 – Peggy Carruthers,
3 – Freda Dixon, 4 – Gwen Hoggarth,
5 – Peggy Brockbank, 6 – Hannah Fleming,
7 – Daisy Lishman, 8 – Elsie Taylor,
9 – Nellie Matthews, 10 – Annie Batty,
11 – Bessie Sharpe.
Back row: 1 – Miss Agnes Burton (teacher),
2 – Harry Lancaster , 3 – George Taylor,
4 – William Matthews,
5 – Jack Gilpin, 6 – Norman Kellett,
7 – Mr. Richard Cragghill.

12. School group 1929.
Front row: 1 – Jack Carruthers, 2 – Amy Harrison,
3 – Olive Hayton, 4 – Marjorie Ellis,
5 – Gladys Kellett, 6 – Harold Ellis.
Second row: 1 – Eileen Kellett, 2 – Margaret Bickley,
3 – Cathy Thornbarrow, 4 – Annie Batty,
5 – Connie Parkinson, 6 – Mary Kellett,
7 – Edna Wilkinson.
Third row: 1 – Elsie Matthews, 2 – Mary Ellis,
3 – Bessie Sharpe, 4 – Nellie Matthews,
5 – Gladys Pearson, 6 – Annie Brockbank,
7 – Margaret Fleming.
Back row: 1 – Mr. Richard Cragghill,
2 – Sally Fleming, 3 – Dick Harrison,
4 – William Matthews, 5 – Norman Kellett,
6 – Geoffrey Harrison, 7 – Eddie Long,
8 – Jack Hayton, 9 – Peggy Brockbank,
10 – Miss Fisher (teacher).

Cartmel Fell

Mrs. Cragghill contributed to the girls' education by taking a weekly class of cookery in her own home. She also taught needlework, and one of her pupils remembers the pain of having a thimble rapped on her head when her stitches were not neat enough.

Until 1914, there was only one classroom, in which children of all ages were taught. Then a second room was constructed, so that another teacher was needed. One of these was Miss Mashiter from Ulverston (Plate 10) who taught at Cartmel Fell about the time of the first world war.

Plates 11, 12, and 13 show groups of schoolchildren in the final four years of Mr. Cragghill's career as headmaster, before he retired in 1931. He left it in good heart, fulfilling a much-needed service to the families of Cartmel Fell. There seemed then no reason for the school to decline.

13. School group 1931.
Front row: *1 – Gladys Kellett, 2 – Olive Hayton, 3 – Annie Metcalfe, 4 – Alice Mallinson.*
Back row: *1 – Ronnie Harrison, 2 – John Mallinson, 3 – Jacky Ridding, 4 – Harry White, 5 – Alan Shepherd.*

14. Mr and Mrs Cragghill on the occasion of their Golden Wedding.

The Final Years

The Education Act of 1944 meant secondary education for all children over eleven, and with families decreasing in numbers too, it was perhaps inevitable that the days of Cartmel Fell school would be numbered. But there are many today for whom the photographs will revive memories of school on the fell, of learning useful crafts; of outings to Morecambe; or of playtime among the rocks and woods around the school.

15. School group in the 1940's.
1 – Lucy Wooff, 2 – Mary Hudson, 3 – Doris Haddow,
4 – Doris Mattinson,
5 – Marjorie Clark, 6 – Frances Scott, 7 – Edna Ellis.
Seated is Adrienne Cleasby.

16. Seaside outing to Morecambe, about 1956.
Front row: *1 - John Crowe, 2 - Celia Hodgson, 3 - Jennifer ?, 4 - Jean Martindale,*
5 - Alison Atkinson, 6 - Stephen Cleasby, 7 & 8 - Ewan & John Wright (twins),
9 - Evelyn Newton.
Back row: *1 - Queenie Cleasby, 2 - Anne Martindale, 3 - Miss Joan Ellison (teacher), 4 - Dorothy Newton, 5 - Pat Newton (small child).*

Cartmel Fell

17. School group in the late 50s.
1. – Celia Hodgson, 2. – John Crowe,
3. – Stephen Cleasby, 4. – Miss Joan Ellison,
5 and 7. – twins Ewan and John Wright from Thorphinsty, 6. – Colin Wright from Goswick Hall (no relation).

18. School Group 1962, sitting above the rock slide.
1 – Paul Whitton, 2 – Susan Penellum,
3 – Sharon O'Flynn, 4 – Paul Barker,
5 – Andrew Stelfox,
6 – Trevor Lupton, 7 – Penny Twigge,
8 – Mrs Caroline Morrison (teacher), 9 – Pat Newton,
10 – Patrick O'Flynn, 11 – Derek Smith,
12 – Joan Dixon,
13 – Roger Van Beevers, 14 – Anthony Clarke,
15 – Michael Johnson.

Schooldays

During the second World War, several evacuees arrived in the neighbourhood. Some were fairly local, having come from Barrow when the shipyards were targeted, and others were from further afield. One of these was Derek Nimmo who came to live at Goswick Hall for a while, and went to school at Cartmel Fell. Former schoolmates have trouble in remembering him; but later he became well-loved for his gentle humour on radio and television. Once, in the programme "Just a Minute", Derek spoke on the topic of Goswick Hall.

One of the last group photographs, taken in 1964, shows that there were only about 20 pupils, and the school once more had only one teacher. Infants and older children were again taught in one room, and the smaller classroom was used for school dinners. These were brought in heated containers from Leven Valley School at Backbarrow, and the van which brought them waited until the containers were washed and returned.

One day, during the hunting season, not a child was to be seen at lunch time. During the morning break they had heard the hunting horn and taken off to follow the hounds. Their teacher was distraught, but they all came back, though well after the appointed dinner hour. Lucy Wooff was then the dinner lady, and had to send the dinner van away without the containers.

By the nineteen seventies, the Education Authority decided that Cartmel Fell school was no longer financially viable; and the children were dispersed among the primary schools of Crosthwaite, Witherslack and Leven Valley. The school closed its doors in 1971.

19. School group 1964.
Front row: 1 – Tom Twigge, 2 – Johnny Twigge, 3 – Gilbert Crowe, 4 – Sharon O'Flynn, 6 – Janet Whitton, 7 – Peter Clarke, 9 – Roger Dixon.
Middle group: 1 – Paul Whitton, 2 – Alan Hewitson, 6 – Joan Dixon, 8 – Christine Rushton.
Back row: 1 – Trevor Lupton, 3 – Derek Smith, 4 – Penny Twigge, 5 – Susan Penellum, 6 – Anne Hewitson.
Several of the children whose names are unknown were only temporarily resident at Ghyll Head.

Cartmel Fell

20. School group 1968.
Front row: 1 – Christine Whitton, 2 – David Cleasby, 3 – David Clarke, 4 – Simon Twigge, 5 – Ian Nicholson, 6 – Ellen Dixon, 7 – Mossop Jopson, 8 – Eric Dixon, 9 – Stuart Holland, 10 – Jane Clarke.
Back row: 1 – Sheena Cleasby, 2 – Gilbert Crowe, 3 – Janet Whitton, 4 – Tom Twigge, 5 – Christine Rushton, 6 – Johnny Twigge, 7 – Peter Clarke, 9 – Roger Dixon.

Schooldays

Ghyll Head Children's Hotel and Nursery School

For some years after the Second War, Ghyll Head House was run as a specialist children's home. It was used mostly by parents who had to live abroad for one reason or another, and whose children had no other home. Some of these children went to local schools such as Cartmel Fell, and others who were at boarding school stayed at Ghyll Head in the holidays. Mrs.O'Flynn, who managed the establishment, was a trained children's nurse, and ran a nursery school for her younger residents and a few local children.

At a time when very few houses could boast central heating, Mrs.O'Flynn made a special point in her prospectus that the house had central heating in cold weather, and the bathrooms were heated all the year round!

21. Ghyll Head House at the time when it was a Children's Hotel.

References
1. *The Diary and Letterbook of the Reverend Thomas Brockbank*. The Chetham Society, 1930. Edited by Trappes & Lomax.
2. *The Cumbria Parishes 1714 - 1725 from Bishop Gastrell's Notitia.*, page 81. Edited by L.A.S.Butler. Published by CW&AAS, Record Series X11, 1998.
3. *Endowed Charities of North Lonsdale, County of Lancaster Parish of Cartmel*. May 21, 1900. HMSO.

2. WORKING LIFE

1. Hay time at Chapel House. John & Polly Fleming and daughter Nelly about 1900.

As in so many other rural parishes, the working lives of the people of Cartmel Fell, the variety of their occupations and the methods they used, have probably changed more in the past fifty years than in the previous two hundred and fifty. The parish registers in Victorian days show that almost three-quarters of the population were engaged in agriculture. The father's occupation is entered in the baptismal record, and right up to the second World War, the pattern was very similar. There were a few wallers and joiners forming the largest tradesmen's group, and one or two shoemakers, with a sprinkling of bobbin-turners and basket-makers. One or two clergy and solicitors brought their children for baptism, and an occasional schoolmaster likewise. Of course, for christenings, the same father might appear more than once in the register, and so the statistics are somewhat clouded; but the register is a fair general indication of occupations.

After 1945, exotic trades begin to appear in the columns of the baptismal register: Photographic Journalist, Furrier, Export Manager, Sculptor and Public Health Inspector – but some of these were not resident on the fell, though many had roots here. No doubt today's census would reveal a further increase in the variety and specialism of the working lives of fell residents.

The photographs in this Chapter have been chosen to try to recapture the rural character of work in bygone days when farming was foremost, but with many others employed in woodland activities, in work on the man-made fabric of the countryside - buildings, walls and roads – and in providing communal services at the shop and public house.

Farming

In Cartmel Fell, as in other upland areas of Britain, the farming year probably changed very little between the 17th century and the mid-20th century. Wartime brought slight changes in crop patterns as the Ministry of Agriculture imposed targets of food production, but as most fields were too rocky to plough, an extra half-acre of turnips was all that some farms could manage. Today, even more than before, farming is predominantly concerned with livestock, especially

Working Life

2. Bait time at Goswick Hall:
Back row: 2 – Jimmy Nicholson, 4 – Fred Taylor, 5 – Richard Walker.
Front row: 2 – Jane Downham, 3 – John Henry Downham, 4 – Mary Walker.

sheep and cattle, rather than crops. The photographs remind us of the very labour-intensive and communal methods in use until mechanisation so transformed farm work.

The greatest changes to take place by the middle of the 20th century were in the methods used at haytime. From earliest times, scything had been a skill needed by all farmers; and whereas grass mowing might have been done with horse power after the invention of a mechanical cutter, the increasing use of tractors brought newer and better machinery to deal with the process of hay-making. Each decade brought bigger and more expensive devices, and instead of the small armies of helpers who used to throng the hay fields, one machine could scale or row-up the hay, and drum mowers took much closer and wider cuts. Gateways needed to be expanded to give access to these ever-larger machines; and then came silage. The dread of a wet summer lessened, and by the 1970s silage pits had arrived on all but the smallest farms, though hay was still needed for sheep and calves. The next step was bagged silage which led to big bales, so that one man with a tractor could move the finished product from the field.

3. The last load on the way back to Thorphinsty. William Taylor with scythe, Isabel and Annie Taylor on top, about 1910.

Cartmel Fell

4. Hartbarrow corn stooks, 1949.

Working Life

5. The Taylors harvesting oats c. 1910.

6. The Taylors' harvest tea-break.

This is all a far cry from the diary of an anonymous female farm servant, whose hay-time work was recorded at Height Farm in 1897[1].

"On July 12th, up at Half past Three o'clock and mowing the little field, and us wemon doing our washing and then going to scale the remainder of the seeds out, getting nine carts and scaling the swaiths in the little field, and raking the seeds at night. Master started cutting the other field, getting up at half past three and finishing it by 8 o'clock, and then setting off to Grange with the Bull, setting the men and turning the other little field, and when getting back, starting to lead the rakings of the seeds getting one–and–a–half carts of it. After that, led six more out of the little field & left the other in platts".

In all, the diary goes on to relate, 91 carts were led from the fields at Height, but Sunday was a day of rest. In that year of 1897, mowing began on July 1st, and the last cartload was housed on Monday the 19th. One wonders how this farm servant had time to write her diary.

In times past, farms were virtually self-sufficient and used to grow fodder crops such as mangolds, swedes, turnips and peas, or a mixture of oats, peas, beans and barley for winter cattle feed. Barley had also been grown for malting, and the remains of a cast-iron malting floor still exists at Burblethwaite Mill.

Oats were the most successful grain crop in the Lakeland climate, and one or two farms still have their griddles for oatcakes, or even the Victorian griddle oven.

Cartmel Fell

7. *The Taylor brothers, James, John, William and Richard, hoeing their prize turnips. The fifth brother, Anthony, was away at the Boer War.*

Working Life

8. Steam threshing at High Tarn Green. John Taylor in centre front.

Cartmel Fell

9. Bert Moon of Great Hartbarrow ploughing in 1947.

Working Life

Many of these photographs remind us of the great importance of horses in farm work, almost as members of the working family. They were still in general use until well after the second World War.

Although farming was a reserved occupation during that War, many of the young men went into the forces and were replaced, first by the newly-formed Women's Land Army, and later to be joined by prisoners-of-war. One such Land Girl, Jo Trickett, came to work at Hare Hill, high on Cartmel Fell, straight from school and a suburban life in Wigan. She still remembers the feeling of anxiety when she set off, carrying her luggage up the long hill from High Newton through the mist. She had no-one to meet her and had no idea how far she had to go.

10. Tommy Dent with horse at Addyfield in about 1910.

Cartmel Fell

12. John and Polly Fleming of Swallowmire taking precautions against the spread of Foot & Mouth disease which had been found at Collinfield in the 1920s.

The official record of the Land Army was written by Vita Sackville-West[2], and the frontispiece is a picture of Jo at Hare Hill with Whitbarrow in the background. This picture became a recruiting poster and could be seen as far afield as Palestine; it was also used for advertising Euthymol toothpaste!

In cattle farming, as in land cultivation, mechanisation has only been comparatively recent. Milking was done by hand, as there was no mains electricity on the fell until 1951 and the area was not completely served until the mid-1960s. Thorphinsty Hall

11. Jo Trickett, Land Army Girl at Hare Hill. Jo was made to stand on the midden to give the photographer a background of Whitbarrow Scar.

Working Life

13. *Peter Lever with brothers James and Colin Wright feeding pet lambs at Goswick Hall, 1950s.*

14. The Downham family of Sow How with their sheep c. 1915.

15. The Taylors of Thorphinsty drying and wrapping fleeces after shearing.

generated its own electricity using a Gilkes turbine in Way Beck in the 1930s; but few other farms aspired to what would be called a milking parlour.

The labour involved in milk production could be even more intensive when there was an outbreak of foot-and-mouth disease. That this has long been a scourge of farmers is evident from William Pearson's memoirs (reference 5, Chapter 6), in which he wrote about a superstitious cure – known as "Need Fire" – for "cattle murrain". The fire had to be kindled out of doors, (preferably by lightning according to some), and infected cattle were driven through the smoke which was supposed to fumigate them. The fire was then quickly gathered up and taken to the next farm where the procedure was repeated. The last place where Pearson went to observe this, in about 1834, was in the narrow lane which leads up to Crosthwaite Church from the Esp Ford road. If the disease was indeed foot-and-mouth, as seems likely, this tramping from one farm to the next would only have spread it further afield.

However it is the sheep that have always been, and still are, the most familiar feature of the farming scene on the fell. Lambing time often brought the "pet lambs" for children to help with; and later on, families and neighbours would give communal "boon-days" to hasten the process of sheep shearing, when the clipping was all done by hand shears. The production of the fleeces was clearly hard for sheep and shearers alike; and Plate 16 recalls the times, fifty and more years ago, when sheep from Cartmel Fell were to be seen along the drove routes into Kendal and beyond. Preparing the sheep for sale was also part of the seasonal work.

Working Life

16. Sheep being driven through the streets of Kendal to the home farm at Hawes after over-wintering on Cartmel Fell, 1950s. *[Photo courtesy of the Margaret Duff Collection.]*

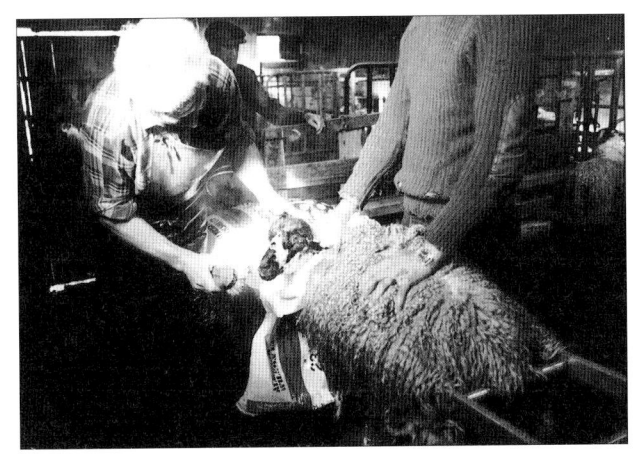

17. "Curly" Cleasby washing a lamb's face prior to the gimmer lambs' sale.

18. Sheila Caldwell with her pullets at Barkbooth, 1947.

Other livestock, once a familiar sight on local farms, are now harder to find. Many a farmer's wife had her own flock of poultry, and turkeys were a common Christmas cash crop.

Market economics and increasingly oppressive regulations have caused a similar decline in pig-farming, with the once-common pig-sty now unoccupied, converted or demolished.

Cartmel Fell

19. Killing a pig in the 19th century, possibly at Cowmire.

20. Tom Newton and turkeys. Lightwood, 1950s.

Working Life

21 a – d. John Strickland and Kenneth Stone harvesting peats, 1930s.

Cartmel Fell

21 e – f.
Peats set out to dry.

Another kind of "harvesting", now discontinued, used to be peat-cutting. Every farm holding would have its own peat "dale", which might have been some distance away, even in another parish. The dales were bequeathed in wills, like other sorts of property, so a widow might leave a dale to her descendants in the place of her birth. The long, narrow peat spades can still be found in old outhouses. With the coming of the railways, coal became accessible to all, and fire grates were installed to produce an updraught; so peat became largely obsolete. But the fuel store at the old school (now the parish hall) on Cartmel Fell is still known as the "peat house".

Working Life

Woodland Work

Apart from agriculture, the woodlands offered the only other major source of employment on the fell. Charcoal had been needed in huge quantities in the past for the iron industry, so the system of coppicing the woodlands every 15 or 16 years was long established. The "coals" were also used for roasting the malting barley in the days when ale or beer was brewed on most farms for everyday consumption; and in the production of gunpowder at Low Wood and elsewhere. Place names such as Collinfield derive from coaling.

22a – e. Charcoal burning at Tower Wood – photos taken by Mr Cragghill in 1904.

a) The burners' (colliers') hut, covered in turf. Tom Lishman (left).
b) Building the stack using swill baskets. The "motty peg" in the centre was later removed and glowing charcoal tipped in to start the "coaling" process.

Cartmel Fell

22. Charcoal burning at Tower Wood (continued)

c) The coaling, showing windshields and the mound covered first with bracken and grass, then sifted earth to prevent air getting in.
d) William Tyson Porter (Mrs Cragghill's brother) helping with "saying" (wetting) and raking the charcoal to hasten cooling. The stack shrank to a third of its original size.

Families on the fell can still remember their forebears who lived the itinerant life of the charcoal men whilst burning was in progress. Although they had homes of their own, and possibly a small farm, they had to live beside their work. The burning had to be tended night and day, with constant attention paid to the wind direction using brushwood screens to protect the stack. A sudden squall could fan the slow smoulder to flame, and the whole stack could burn to ashes unless damped down. The burners lived in temporary huts made of poles covered with sods, but with a permanent fireplace. These hearths can still be found all over the fell, but little else remains.

It was a delightful summer excursion for the children of these men to visit the camp, taking with them all sorts of goodies from home, and one of the photographs shows an array of baskets, may be filled with provisions. Sometimes the boys might sleep overnight on bracken beds in the charcoal burners' hut, so children learned the principles of construction to build their own play-huts. Dorothy Newton remembers an improvement she and her siblings made. They lined *their* roof with newspaper to divert the continuous drizzle of grit from the sods.

Working Life

22. Charcoal burning at Tower Wood (continued)

e) Bagging the charcoal.

As well as charcoal, the coppice woods provided all manner of products, from baskets and besoms to ships' fenders and tent pegs. In Victorian days, new plantations were established by the Wakefields at Lamb How and Rankthorns for pit-props, and a letter survives from their agent, James Holme[3]:

> "Sir, Mr. James Harrison was over yesterday and I went with him to view the prop wood. I offered it to him at the price we agreed, viz. for yours from Lamb How and Rankthorns to be delivered at Windermere at 26 shillings per hundred yards".

The bark was stripped from the prop wood before sale, and was bagged and sold separately, and as with oak bark it was used for tanning. The trees were felled in June when the rising sap aided the stripping. Youngsters could earn a useful shilling or two in helping to rive the bark from the timber. "Barkbooth" as a house name indicates the site of such industry.

Arthur Ransome, who lived on Cartmel Fell between the wars (see Chapter 6), wrote about two charcoal burners, called Old and Young Billy[4]. Young Billy was a grandfather in his seventies, but Old Billy was 94 and still working. They may well have been two generations of Lishmans, a local family engaged in woodland work and who lived at Bryan Beck, Bridge House and Bowland Bridge. In *"Swallows and Amazons"*, Arthur Ransome wrote of these charcoal burners keeping an adder in a cigar box "for luck" – but the adder probably didn't think it was so lucky!

Although just before the second World War there was a requirement for charcoal for use in gas masks, the War itself all but destroyed the coppice woods because of the drain on manpower, so the trees grew tall. The able-bodied young men went into the forces, unless they worked in a reserved occupation such as farming; so the old woodsmen just got older. By the war's end, the number of managed coppice woods had declined sharply; and charcoal burning as a way of life was finished.

By the 1960s, another old woodland craft was dying. The traditional oak swill, which was used for almost every farm purpose, was on the verge of extinction. It had been made in the Furness area for generations, and several such craftsmen appear in the Cartmel Fell parish registers. "Chippy" Winder from Greenthorn

Cartmel Fell

23. Not everyone could afford a horse! 1930s.

24. Lengthsmen Tommy Crowe and Billy Lishman working near Bowland Bridge.

was one of the last basket-makers in Cartmel Fell, and was a friend to all the school children who would call in for a chat on their way home.

Today, however, all is not quite lost of these old woodland activities. In recent years a renewal of interest in country crafts has led to a new generation of swill-makers who learned the process just before the old skills were lost. Now, as well as courses and centres for coppicing and its related activities, one can even find among the Furness fells (though not yet on Cartmel Fell) good quality charcoal being produced, but now using steel kilns, to serve the growing market for barbecue fuel.

Public Service and Building Work

The creation of district councils in the second half of the 19th century brought a change in public services. The maintenance of roads, bridges and drains, together with Law and Order and the care of the poor, had been parish obligations until this time. The officers for the year were paid for their expenses, but received no

25. Work in progress on replacement farm buildings at Hodge Hill, 1904.

Working Life

salary for the posts of Constable, Grave*, Overseer of the Poor and Chapel Warden. The officers were appointed on an annual rotational basis, each yeoman taking his turn. In practice, this meant that very few yeomen needed to do any particular job more than once. Occasionally, the same name crops up several times in succession, and an accompanying note in the ledger shows that the office is being held as a substitute for another (probably wealthier, or perhaps unhealthier, or even absent) landowner. In these cases we might assume that money changed hands privately.

Once these responsibilities were transferred to County Councils, a new type of employment opened up. There were local policemen, and road men known as "lengthsmen" who cut back the verges, cleared the drains and swept up leaves. Now that we have to contact the police in Penrith to report a local crime, or to clear out a roadside drain ourselves, those earlier times seem like a golden age.

Building and walling have always provided a small amount of employment on the Fell. Plate 25 records a notable building achievement from nearly a century ago. The impressive structure at Hodge Hill was built to replace farm buildings destroyed by a fire, thought to have been started deliberately by an aggrieved ex-employee.

26. *James Herd dry stone walling, 1990s.*

Dry stone walling has been a craft which has contributed much to the appearance of the Lakeland countryside, since the enclosures 200 years ago, and the old skills are still practised. It is a very labour-intensive process, and therefore expensive; so many stretches of wall have sadly fallen into disuse or been replaced by post and wire. However, thanks to grants, some walls are now being reinstated.

*North Country name, now obsolete, for Steward.

Cartmel Fell

27. Bowland Bridge shopkeepers Mary Walker and Violet Parkinson with Mary Walker, junior, 1930s.

28. John Wood at Bowland Bridge Post Office and shop, 1990s. [Photo courtesy of the Westmorland Gazette.]

Other Services to the Community

Those who work at the village shop(s) and inns have long played a vital part in the communal life of the Fell. From the mid 19th century, two shops had existed, one attached to each public house. At Strawberry Bank, a grocery was opened by Margaret Tyson in the room adjoining the road. Just below, in the valley bottom but in a different parish and another county, the Walker family were landlords of Bowland Bridge. The Hare & Hounds provided instant refreshment, and the shop across the road sustained its customers with goods of all kinds, such as paraffin, yeast and pop. The extraordinary family of Walkers (see also Chapter 5) seemed to need no sleep, and a local resident well remembers refreshing himself with half a pint of ale on his way to work at 6 a.m. The shop, too, was open at all hours. If you were returning home after a night out at 2 a.m. and running short of paraffin, then Mrs. Walker might rise from washing the floor to serve you. Her grand-daughter, Connie Parkinson, recalls returning from dances in the early hours, longing for her bed, and still being expected to serve passing customers!

The Strawberry Bank grocer ceased to exist around 1870, though the inn continues to this day. The Bowland Bridge shop-cum-post-office flourishes, after a short break in the 1970s. There was a change of ownership when Mrs. Parkinson (*née* Walker) retired and Bert Lever took over, assisted from time to time by Mrs. Morrison, the schoolmistress at Cartmel Fell. Bert continued the tradition of being open at somewhat unusual hours. When, on one wintry January night, the snow-plough came down over the

Working Life

bridge to turn in the car-park of The Hare & Hounds, Bert was heard to shout: "Doos't want owt, afore ah shoot oop?" The time was quarter to three in the morning!

When Bert retired, a few years passed until the shop was bought in 1983 by John and Molly Wood, who have steadily improved and enlarged the premises. Today it is the Post Office, general store, filling station and cafe, and as such provides a much-used social meeting-point for the local community.

The two public houses likewise have served the community well, and today bring visitors from afar to enjoy their many delights. One local tradition, however, ceased when in 1974 Westmorland and Lancashire-North-of-the-Sands were merged into the new county of Cumbria. Previously, the Hare & Hounds, being in Westmorland, had closed at 10 p.m. whereas the pub on Strawberry Bank kept to the Lancashire closing time of 10.30. So it was a common sight to see determined drinkers cover the quarter mile up-hill as fast as possible to enjoy a final "one for the road" in the Mason's Arms.

Finally, Plate 29 recalls another kind of communal work which used to be carried out differently, but certainly no less efficiently, than today. The postman who walked many miles each day, starting from High Newton whatever the weather, not only delivered the mail, but also sold stamps from a little roadside hut below Strawberry Bank, where he ate his lunch. The postman, James Long, is still remembered with affection; and it was he who composed the poem "Tory Social" quoted in Chapter 4.

29. *James Long, the postman and poet, delivering to School House.*

References
1. WDY 462. Access No.2506. Kendal RO.
2. *The Women's Land Army.* V. Sackville-West. Now in reprint from The Imperial War Museum. £17.50
3. BDB/5. Barrow RO.
4. *Swallows and Amazons.* Arthur Ransome. Jonathan Cape, 1931.

3. WORSHIP

To the casual visitor, there are few obvious signs that religion has played a significant role in life on the fell. What evidence there is must be sought off the beaten track; and shows that worship, both orthodox and dissenting, has indeed played its part in this far-flung community.

So if it were not for a few modest signposts, St. Anthony's Church could easily be missed altogether, tucked away on the eastern slopes of the fell surrounded by woodland. In fact, both geographically and for historical reasons, its position is very logical.

Likewise, the existence of the old Meeting House and nearby Burial Ground of the Religious Society of Friends, high on the remote fell, is known to rather few, but testifies to the strong support which Quakerism enjoyed, especially in the 17th and 18th centuries. Thus in unobtrusive ways, religious belief has found expression in local worship for nearly five hundred years past.

The "Chapel of Ease"

In the 15th century the men of power and wealth hereabouts were the Briggs of Cowmire Hall and the Knipes of Burblethwaite Hall. As far as control went, the Knipes had the edge, as Burblethwaite was a little manor. The Lord of the Manor collected annual dues from his farmholders, both in money and in kind, together with boon service. However, this did not amount to very much in the Knipes' case, as they had only the land which stretched to the south, encompassing perhaps five farms. The river Winster was their boundary, and that of the county also, Cartmel Fell being in old Lancashire.

The Briggs' lands were on the other side of the river, technically in the parish of Crosthwaite in Westmorland. It is hard to imagine how the two families came together to propose and finance a new church, because documents showed that they were continually at war for most of the Tudor period. A very pressing need must have been the reason; probably the fact that to get to the Mother Church of Cartmel meant a journey of more than two hours on

1. St Anthony's in spring.

Worship

foot, and many people must have been unable to undertake it. The unenclosed common where the new chapel was built is almost equidistant from Cowmire and Burblethwaite Halls.

St. Anthony is the patron saint of hermits, swineherds and charcoal-burners, and is usually depicted with a T-staff, a bell and a pig beside him. Since charcoal-burners' pitsteads can be found all over Cartmel Fell, St. Anthony was a very fitting choice of patron for the district. Technically, St. Anthony's is a Chapel of Ease, so called because it eased the lot of would-be churchgoers, for most of whom it would be very much nearer than Cartmel.

2. The Briggs family pew in 1875.

In a deposition made by Anthony Knipe in 1561[1], he states that his father William and others erected the chapel about fifty-five years earlier. He also said that twelve discreet men of the parish collected monies for the priest's stipend and repairs to the fabric of the church, but earlier in the 16th century the salary was taken care of by Robert Briggs. In his will of 1520, he left 33s. 4d. for life, to John Holme Briggs, priest, providing he took no wages from the township and boarded with Robert's son Thomas.

Various sums of money were bequeathed to the church over a long period, and gifts of church furniture. Robert Briggs gave a chalice and pese (or kneeler) to Cartmel Priory in 1504, but only on condition that they were lent to Cartmel Fell chapel at Easter for communion, or, as he put it, "*To Housel with*". In 1531, Thomas Smyth of Pontefract left a bequest of "*One Chales, in valow XLs.*" to the "*Chapell of Sanct. Antony*"[2].

The salaries of the early incumbents were very small indeed. For instance in 1704 it was £8 10s. 2d., later augmented by the interest from small bequests[3]. Several separate grants of £200 from Queen Anne's bounty were awarded to the chapel in the 18th and 19th centuries, and these sums were laid out on land. Small estates were bought, the first being Simpson Ground, and the tenant's rent went towards the curate's salary.

At various periods, the fabric of the chapel was in a near ruinous state, and in 1708 was said to be "*out of repair and unfurnished*"[4]. Strangely, this was only ten years after the new triple-decker pulpit had been

Cartmel Fell

4. Royal Coat of Arms of George III. Erected in 1778 at a cost of £3 14s. 0d. as an expression of loyalty to the Sovereign.

been clothiers and wool merchants. The crucifix which once hung on the rood screen is now in Kendal museum, and is one of only three surviving from such an early date, that is, the late 15th century. The other two are Welsh[5].

3. The inside of the church, c. 1850, showing the three-decker pulpit with window behind, and the Knipe family pew.

installed. The placing of this pulpit and the enclosed pews of Burblethwaite Hall and Cowmire Hall illustrates the old rivalries. The two families, Briggs and Knipe, had their elaborately carved box pews face to face across the aisle. The Briggs family had turned the old rood screen into their domain when the screen was dismantled at the Reformation. Maybe they had paid for the screen when the church was built some forty years earlier, and the sections were turned around to enclose an area, as seen in Plate 2, which had a table in the centre, and is thought to have been the schoolroom of the day. The carving is Flemish in style, and incorporates a tenter hook and the letter M for the mercer's guild, the Briggs having

Worship

6. The parish clerk making announcements from the sundial in the churchyard.

5. The minister and the shoemaker sitting on the tombstone under the east window.

Cartmel Fell

7. The church in the 1870s, recently re-roofed, with Revd. William Summers, Vicar of St Anthony's 1867-1909, and his dog.

The pulpit is on the south wall in the centre of the church, with the date 1698 on the door. In order for the reader to see his text, a small window (which can be seen in Plate 3) was inserted high up on the wall, and the accounts for making this window still survive. It took thirteen days work, at a cost of thirteen shillings in 1697[6].

8,9. The church in the early 1900s showing Harvest Festival decorations.

The Church in the 18th and 19th Centuries

Although Cartmel Fell had been granted permission for its Chapel of Ease in 1504, the parishioners still had to go to Cartmel for all their baptisms, weddings and funerals. It is hard to imagine how folk had previously managed to transport corpses when roads were almost non-existent. Probably sleds were sometimes used, or else they were put on pack saddles. It was over two hundred years before the Bishop of Chester licensed the chapel and graveyard at Cartmel Fell for burials in 1712. Stockdale tells us[7] that St. Anthony's had two biers, both of oak, and a load in themselves; and it is known that dozens of men were invited to country funerals, simply to provide relays of coffin bearers. Perhaps a series of bad winters or wet summers caused the decision to petition the Bishop for a burial licence. Much later in the 18th century, marriages and baptisms were licensed too, but the dues for all these services were still paid to Cartmel Priory.

Some glimpses of Church activities in the 19th century can be found in drawings by Bertha Newcombe, which can be seen in the church, and are shown in Plates 3, 5 and 6.

10. Revd. Thomas Price, vicar 1909-1916.

11. Interior of the church before the 1911 restoration.

12. View of the church after the 1911 restoration. The oil lamps were not replaced by electricity until the early 1960s.

Cartmel Fell

13. View to the east, showing stained glass and the panelling behind the altar made by Hubert Simpson in 1936.

In this rural parish, harvest festivals were an important annual event, celebrated with much decoration of the church, as seen in Plates 8 and 9, taken in the early 1900s.

Restoration of the Church in 1911

The weather and lack of funding caused further deterioration to the fabric of St.Anthony's in the 19th century. When Thomas Price arrived as the new incumbent in 1909, he began an active campaign to improve matters. The whole church is built on a slope, and over the centuries, soil had washed down the fell and piled up at the western end, until what had once been a doorway became merely a window in the belfry tower, with four or five feet of earth against

Incumbents at St.Anthony's Church

1504	- 1520	William Rawlinson
1520	- ?	John Holme Briggs
1559	- 1561	John Wilson
1585	- 1599	John Copeland
1605		Robert Dowson
1608	- 1648	Gilbert Steill
1649	- 1658	John Brooke
1659	- 1660	George Inman
1675	- 1877	George Stainton
1680	- 1699	John Mac Dowell
1700	- 1703	William Myles
1703	- 1706	Jonah Walker
1707	- 1710	Thomas Hotblack
1712	- 1714	William Sandys
		(buried in the Church)
1715	- 1758	George Walker
1766	- 1767	Nelson Braithwaite
1770		William Danson
1776	- 1779	John Birkett
1782	- 1790	Thomas Clarke
1790	- 1827	John Allenby
1827	- 1828	William Wilson
1829	- 1861	Robert B. Cockerton
1862	- 1867	Thomas Carter
1867	- 1909	William Summers
1909	- 1916	Thomas Price
1916	- 1933	George Clayton
1934	- 1939	Charles Last
1939	- 1943	Frank Cowburn
1943	- 1951	G. Beresford-Hope
1951	- 1962	John Sell
1962	- 1975	Theodore Barrett
1975	- 1995	Kenneth Partington
1996		William Greetham

Worship

14. The dedication of the War Memorial in April 1924, attended by the King's Own Royal Border Regiment.

> This stone and Lych Gate were erected to the memory of the Officers and Men of this Parish who fell in the Great War.
>
> Wm. H.B.Higgin Birket, John J.Gilpin, Thomas S.I.Hall, Joseph Hott, Harry H.Lishman, Henry Matthews, Luke Sowerby, Alfred E.Whitfield, Anthony Willan, John Willan, Joseph.S.Willan
>
> Lest we forget
>
> Also 1939-1945
> R.A. Branson, J.A. Brocklebank

the wall. The rendering was rotten, and the windows a mis-matched jig-saw of stained glass. It is evident from several sources that repairs to the windows had been effected from a box of assorted stained glass kept for the purpose. The windows themselves may have been salvaged from Cartmel Priory, for they pre-date the building of St.Anthony's, and do not conform to its flat-arched Tudor window frames. The central portion of the Priory was roofless for eighty years after the Dissolution, so the windows must have suffered greatly. It seems that some early conservationist turned Cartmel's misfortune to Cartmel Fell's advantage. Bowness Church is said to have benefited in the same way.

Plate 11 shows the church interior before Thomas Price's restoration. He sent the windows to Knowles of York to be re-arranged, but even so, there are still many pieces missing. The central portion of the east window shows the seven sacraments, radiating from the wounds of Christ, and to the left is an almost complete window showing St.Anthony himself. On the right is a bishop with a chain on his wrist, depicting either St. Leonard or St. Peter in Chains.

Visitors will notice the rather charming boards which display the Ten Commandments, the Creed and the Lord's Prayer. There are accounts for the re-lettering of these in 1794, and for putting them into new frames. The total for the work and the transport from Kendal came to £7 14s. 5d. The busty little cherubs which decorate the top of one panel are very similar in style to those at Cartmel Priory, so they must have been a speciality of a Kendal signwriter of the day.

The present appearance of the church clearly owes much to the efforts and enthusiasm of Thomas Price who achieved so much in his relatively short incumbency. His successor was George Clayton, who was the incumbent when the War Memorial was dedicated in 1924.

St. Anthony's Church Today

Today, the church has to share its vicar (Plate 15) with three other parishes, but it has a steady stream of visitors from far and wide. Footpaths converge here from all over the fell, first trodden by farmers of long ago, but now followed by walkers and other visitors to enjoy the rural tranquillity of St. Anthony's church. Sadly, the very few furnishings possessed by the church were stolen in recent years. First, the parish chest was taken from the belfry, and also the Bishop's chair. Most recently, the replacement chair was stolen but recovered. The ancient pitch-pipe, seen in Plates 3 and 16 was taken from the vestry in 1999.

In an even more bizarre piece of criminal activity, a tomb in the churchyard was used as the hiding place for picture frames stolen from Holker Hall in 1999. The paintings had been removed, presumably in the graveyard, and the frames deposited inside a large "chest" type monument. Maybe the robbers thought that the frames would languish there till domesday, but a sharp-eyed lady noticed that the slab top of the tomb was slightly crooked when she arranged some flowers on it. Happily, the paintings have since been recovered and returned to Holker Hall.

Worship

19. Friends Meeting House at Height c. 1900.

15. (Opposite) Canon Bill Greetham, flanked by churchwardens Oliver Barratt (left) and Anthony Clarke, 1997.

16. (Opposite) Items once held in the church: Cromwellian pewter flagon 1635-40. Pre-guild date. Used at communion. 18th century oak offertory plate. An original door key. The blackthorn pitch-pipe, c. 1700, which gave the key for the singing of hymns.

Non-Conformist Worship

The Religious Society of Friends had a strong presence on Cartmel Fell in the 17th and 18th centuries. At first they met in the farmhouses of their followers, one of these being Lawrence Newton. A marriage was performed at his house in 1660, and when he died in 1676, he left a will bequeathing land and money to build a permanent Meeting House for the Quakers, as they came to be called.

This was one of the earliest custom-built Meeting Houses, as at that time all gatherings of non-conformists were prohibited and fineable. The date of 1677 over the entrance porch at Height shows that the Friends lost no time in constructing their Meeting House, and accounts survive which show that the whole enterprise cost £106 9s. 7d. The greatest expenditure was the men's wages, amounting to £25 14s. 3d. At this period also, a Burial Ground was created across the road, which is still occasionally used today.

Until the Act of Toleration in 1689, the Quakers who assembled at Height were sorely persecuted by the Establishment, for non-payment of tithes and for meeting together. If the offenders could not pay in cash, their goods were seized, and these included cattle, sheep and even basic utensils such as kettles and dishes.

Thomas Preston of Holker was the tithe farmer for the Bishop of Chester, and these tiresome, unyielding Quakers must have been a festering thorn in his flesh. All he wanted was to be rid of them and instal tenants who submitted to the old customs, paid their tithes, doffed their hats and let him get on with his job. It was never so. When one of their number was sent to Lancaster jail, as happened frequently, the Friends supported the family who were left without a breadwinner. As the reign of William and Mary progressed, toleration of a more general kind began to extend. It was about this time that a non-conformist academy was established by Richard Frankland at Hartbarrow, about a mile north of the church. Now also the Quakers could meet more openly, and they built a cottage adjoining the Meeting House for the use of a farmer-cum-caretaker.

One of these was Jonathan Wilson, and one of his ledgers survives which records his life from 1727 until 1780. This is one of many documents relating to Height Meeting which were discovered in 1996 in a

Cartmel Fell

18. Andrew Watson, 1997, playing the organ, which was hand-pumped in pre-electricity days.

17. St. Anthony in the east window of the church.

Worship

nearby farm and these are now reproduced at Kendal Record Office[8]. Jonathan Wilson kept a list of visiting Friends, and during his stewardship he named more than 200 men and women who had come to Height from as far afield as Virginia and Maryland, as well as the four corners of England. He kept a few cows, but his main enterprise was chair making, as his accounts show. In the garden of the cottage is a shelter for bee skeps, an open-fronted building with slots for shelves; so honey and bees-wax candles were probably a sideline.

The numbers attending Height meeting dwindled during the 19th century, but a description of the interior of the house was written by Mary Wakefield around the beginning of the last century[9]. She said the floor was painted green and the benches were unpainted. Two men and a woman sat facing the gathering on a slightly raised platform, with the men on one side, the women on the other.

The meeting closed in the nineteen twenties, and for a while the large room was used as a hay barn. It is now a private house. The original vellum indentures, with the names of the first Trustees, were exchanged when the Meeting House was purchased from the Friends. All the original panelling has been retained, and the unusually large windows make it a bright and tranquil place to live.

20. Anthony Prickett, the Meeting House caretaker, about 1900.

References

1. *Duchy of Lancs Pleadings, Elizabeth. XLVIII*, B.21. C&W Transactions, 1912. p.285. John F.Curwen, F.S.A. F.R.I.B.A.
2. Surtees Soc. Vol 79. *Testamentia Eboricensia*, Vol 5. p.302.
3. *Bishop Gastrell's "Notitia Cestrensis" of 1724*. Chetham Soc. Vol 22. p.501.
4. C&W Transactions, 1912. p.288. John F.Curwen, F.S.A. F.R.I.B.A.
5. C&W Transactions, 1982. p.125. G.A.Behrens. *Conservation Work on the Cartmel Fell Figure of Christ*.
6. Kendal R.O. WPR/4.
7. James Stockdale, *Annals of Cartmel*.
8. Kendal R.O. WDY/462.
9. Mary Wakefield, *Cartmel Priory and Sketches of North Lonsdale*. H.T.Mason, Grange, 1909.

4. SOCIAL LIFE

The photographs of social activities in this Chapter were nearly all taken out-of-doors. Of course, before the advent of the flash-bulb and high-speed film, indoor snapshots were inevitably hazardous; but their scarcity in this collection is also because so much of social and communal life on and around Cartmel Fell was to be found in the open air.

1. Anthony Chapman with the Coniston Foxhounds.

Social Life

Cartmel Fell Hunt Charter

This Charter granted to the Mayor Recorder Alderman Bailif & Burgess of the Corperation of Cartmel Fell, by William the Conqueror in the year of our Lord 1066 for the zeal and glorious behavaiour to the Crown; he thought meet to grant to ther Corperation by their own Desire a free right to chuse a mayor and such other Officers as should seem to them most meet for the better regulating their laws hearafter mentioned. The levying of fines and applying them to such uses as seemeth most good and right, to them; the bounds of their Corperation being laid out by Hundreds and Tythings; that is to say, it begins at Lyndeth and so to Belman Landing, down by the waterside to the Townhead in Stavley, from there over the Mountains to Bowland Bridge, so cross the forest to guilpin Bridge in Crook, this is to be their hunting ground unmolested on this Day where they may hunt with large Dogs the Fox, Cat, Mart etc. and with the Beagels the fine sporting here and after they be tired to go to the Corperation hall and chuse a Mayor and other Officers for the good order of the above Corperation; that is to say every new Mayor to pay 1s. new Recorder not less than 6d. Alderman 4d. freemen not less than 3d. Fines to be levied are every person getting drunk to pay 4d. or put in limbo the space of one hour. Any persons quraling each party to pay 4d.; for every oath 2d.; all Batchelors above 27 to pay 4d. every year they keep unmarried unless they freely confess their Design was to marry but always rejected.

So God Save the King.

(signed) James Wilson
Underbarrow.

An excerpt from the Huntsman's Charter.
Far Right: A transcript of the Huntsman's Charter.

The above is a transcript of an old document written about the year 1810. Another version has come to light among "Papers belongin To Stroberry Bank Mair hunt Cartmelfell", which elaborates, and extends to women, the system of fines for improper behaviour…

51

Cartmel Fell

..........he who spills drink into his neighbour's pocket and he who singes his neighbour's hair with his pipe are to be fined 2d. each; And all unmarried women who go A gossiping more than 6 Days in one week are to be fined 6d. and all married men or bachelors who Keep them company and hold them up with their tittle tattle and nonsense are to be fined 2d. the fines to be levied and collected by the Mayor or his order and expeinded on ale spirits & Tobacco to make glad the hearts of our loyal and loving subjects.

An excerpt from the other version of the Huntsman's Charter.

2. The Lunesdale Harriers at Hodge Hill in the late 1940s. Mrs Johnson on the left.

Country Sports

It would probably be true to say that most country sports which are now viewed as leisure activities arose out of need. The enjoyment of hunting, shooting and fishing still runs deep in the veins of many countrymen, and there is the satisfaction of knowing that there is one less fox in the district – still very pertinent in this area of sheep-rearing. If farmers are suffering heavy lamb losses, they may call in the hunt for more than sporting reasons.

One huntsman of Cumbrian renown was Anthony Chapman, who was born at the Hare and Hounds (where else?) in Bowland Bridge. He was huntsman of the Coniston Hunt from 1944 until 1976, having been a shepherd earlier in the war. He killed his first fox on Cartmel Fell on 25th November 1944.

There are still regular meets of the Coniston and Lunesdale hounds on the Fell during the winter, and the followers come from far and wide. Nowadays a few fit and young people follow on foot, but there is a growing contingent of the not-so-young who get as close as possible to the action by car. We have no records of the origins of fox-hunting on the Fell, but it was obviously a well-loved social tradition by the end of the 18th century. A piece of paper survives from this time, written no doubt with tongue in cheek, and mimicking a legal document.(See previous page).

Social Life

Part of manuscript of "A Favourite New Hunting Piece".

Goswick Hall Beagles

Tis of Goswick Hall Beagles I'm going to relate
Tis to these gallant hounds, many hares owe their fate,
There was Fanner & Fencer & Frolic as well
Which are the best, takes a good man to tell.

Tally-ho, Tally-ho
Hark for'ard good hounds
Tally-ho.

There's one I've missed out and Comrade's his name
Now he is a hound of fair hunting fame,
For a hare to outwit him is not in its power
He can make a hare run many miles in the hour.

Tally-ho etc.

These four little hounds are owned by John Barrow
He's a grand sporting man and you'll ne'er find his marrow.
With him for the huntsman and Rhoda for't whip
These fleet little hounds over't fell fairly slip.

Tally-ho etc.

Now here's luck to the huntsman, his whip and his pack,
And hope that good fortune will lie in their track.
For hunting's the sport to which sporting men cling
From early in autumn to early in spring.

Tally-ho etc.`

3. Harold Hodgson, the auctioneer, singing hunting songs in the Mason's Arms, Strawberry Bank.

Cartmel Fell

4. A shooting party outside the Hare & Hounds, Bowland Bridge.
1 – Myles Cockerton, 3 – Mrs Bentley, 7 & 8 – Mr & Mrs Smith, 9 – Wilfred Bentley.

5. Richard Taylor of Thorphinsty and his future brother-in-law with their ferrets.

Earlier in the 20th century, a pack of beagles was kept at Goswick Hall by John Barrow, and a song in their praise is still remembered. Plate 2, taken during the 1940s, shows the stirrup cup being served to the Lunesdale Harriers. At the end of a day's hunting, the company would repair to a local inn and sing the traditional hunting songs. The tune for "A Favourite New Hunting Piece" was recently discovered at Bowland Bridge in a book of manuscript music which had belonged in 1815 to Henry Hird of Moor How. The tune may well have originated locally, but its composer, and the instrument(s) for which it was written, are as yet unknown.

Another necessary occupation was rabbit control, using ferrets and guns. The Taylors of Thorphinsty Hall derived a considerable part of their income from the sale of rabbits.

Many sporting activities, such as the 1930s shooting party seen in Plate 6, began and ended with a drink or two. The five "gentlemen" seen are those remembered in another local ditty, about a barrel of beer.

Song of the Beer Barrel

On the fifth of October five gentlemen came
To the Great Gillhead Tower, shooting the game.
A week before that, or a fortnight maybe,
They had brought a beer barrel to settle, you see.

Chorus
Then hurrah for the sportsmen of fame and renown,
Who came from that famous old Windermere town,
They laugh and they joke and they sing and they dance,
And always send forward their drink in advance.

Now the barrel was placed on a stock strong and broad
In a hut they intended to make their abode,
And one of them remarked "That job's very well done,
I can now get a drink if I'm dry when I come".

Then some other people, the story thus runs,
Who shoulder their axes more often than guns,
Found it and vowed they'd have it to tap,
For it would be a sin to let it go flat.

Now the sportsmen arrived at the wood in due course,
And scarcely had time to look after the horse,
As each one declared he was awfully dry
To sample the barrel they soon had a try.

Now when they found the barrel was dry
The look on their faces to describe I'll ne'er try,
And the words used, when their anger got vent
Your imagination I'll leave to invent.

I hope from my song you will learn to be wise
If you happen to go where they're not civilised.
Be advised by the people, these five sportsmen say so;
Remember you'd best take your liquor when you go.

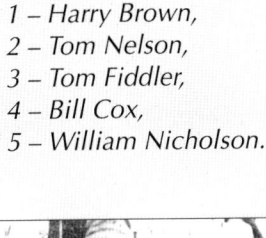

6. The five thirsty sportsmen:
1 – Harry Brown,
2 – Tom Nelson,
3 – Tom Fiddler,
4 – Bill Cox,
5 – William Nicholson.

Cartmel Fell

Competitive Sports

The Taylor family, of whom more is recorded in Chapter 5, produced sportsmen with other skills. John Taylor senior, of Thorphinsty Hall, was a notable bare-knuckle boxer in the 19th century; and his descendant, John Taylor junior, engaged in the ever-popular Cumberland and Westmorland Wrestling, in which the special costumes are such a distinctive feature.

Another individual sport born from necessity is sheepdog trialling, and shepherds who are good with dogs compete locally and nationally. One of today's renowned trainers is Alan Foster of Sow How, who in 1999 was an English and International Judge of sheepdog trials.

7. *John Taylor of High Tarn Green, c. 1910. The embroidery was done by his sisters.*

8. *Alan Foster with Flint, behind Sow How in 1994.*
[Photo courtesy of the Westmorland Gazette.]

Social Life

9. *Bowland Bridge football club, winners of the Dutton Cup, 1950s.*
Standing: *1 – William Matthews, 2 – Walter Holt, 3 – Henry Airey, 4 – Derek Birch, 5 – Gordon Gregg, 6 – Alan Pearson, 7 – Neville Holland, 8 – Jim Wright, 9 – Bill Barker.*
Kneeling: *1 – "Curly" Cleasby, 2 – Bill Moffatt, 3 – Alan Leake, 4 – Ken Park, 5 – Fred Greenhow.*

Team sports have also flourished from time to time. After the second World War the local men-folk organised a football team; and Jim Wright tells how some of the football club members decided to start a cricket club. At their first home game, they dismissed Kendal Jubilee Club for a mere 29 runs, largely thanks to Derek Cleasby's bowling, and soundly defeated them after hitting a ball into a large patch of nettles. While the Kendal players gingerly searched for it, the Bowland Bridge batsmen continued to run! The Kendalians declined to play again and the Bowland Bridge team disbanded due to lack of opponents. The football club's funds had been used to buy the cricket equipment, so it, too, closed down at this time.

Cartmel Fell

10. Dickie Walker fishing with the children of Bowland Bridge – Walkers, Lishmans and Pearsons. Mrs Walker and Mrs Lishman are on the bridge, about 1910.

Social Life

11. A foggy morning's skating on Podnet Moss, December 1976.

Cartmel Fell

Activities for Children

Early in the 1900s very little was organised for children to do in their leisure hours, and they were no doubt happy to spend time sitting along the wall of Bowland Bridge, and perhaps try to catch the little trout swimming below. There was a Boy Scout troop in the 1920s, but most entertainments were home-grown. A game that has virtually disappeared was "spell and knurr" which was played with a small ball or other object which had to be hit after launching from a swinging platform. Another version of this game was called "guinea pig". The Girls' Friendly Society used to meet in the school in the evening, and dancing classes were held in the upstairs room of the Hare and Hounds.

12. Sports Days on the Fell involve young and old:
1 – David Clarke,
2 – David Cleasby, 3 – Billy Hodgson,
5 – "Curly" Cleasby, 6 – Gwen Rushton,
7 – John Kitching, 9 – Rosalyn Kitching,
10 – Martin Jackson, 11 – Bill Adam,
12 – Bert Cleasby, 14 – Bob Foulerton,
15 – Lesley Wright, 17 Fran Ogilvy.
On the pole: George Clarke & Trevor Lupton. 1977

13. From the right: 1 – Sue Smith, 2 - Linda Hodgson, 5 – James Smith , 6 – Mike Smith, 7 – Millie Lupton. 1981.

Social Life

Thanks to the 1960s "baby boom", there were, by the late 1970s, enough 7-14 year olds for a small youth club. Organised by the parents and ably led by "Curly" Cleasby, it met fortnightly for table tennis and pool in the winter, and for games of shinty on fine summer evenings. On at least one frosty weekend, the shinty sticks were used for an impromptu game of ice hockey up on the Fell at Podnet Moss. The youth club also started the tradition of the Cartmel Fell bonfire party for November 5th, and organised

14 & 15. Royal Wedding Barbecue and Fancy Dress.
14. 1– Dorothy Grant, 4 – Tom Cartwright, (as a lady),
5 – Jenny Cartwright, 6 – Louise Tongue, 7 – Frank Mills.

15. 1 – James Smith, 7 – Alan Foster, 8 – Nancy Matthews,
9 – Alec Smith, 10 – Mike Smith, 11 – Ruth Smith.

Cartmel Fell

16. School Christmas Party 1964.
Left to right *(where known): Penny Twigge, Gillian Holland, Derek Mason, Johnny Twigge, Janet Whitton (dark hair), with Alan Hewitson behind. Jane Clarke (front), with Ossie (Tom) Twigge behind. Gilbert Crowe, with Joan Dixon and David Mason behind. Bridie Blades (behind donkey whose name was Tennyson), Pat Newton, Michael Smith (the tallest), Paul Whitton, Anne Hewitson, Sally & Simon Twigge, Christine Rushton (with hand on donkey), Christine Smith with Derek Smith behind and Ellen & Roger Dixon.*
Adults: *Laura Hodgson, Gladys Crowe, Jim and Eileen Lupton.*

summer sports days, with a variety of competitive events. Other highlights included a barbecue and children's fancy dress competition, to celebrate the Royal Wedding in 1981.

Latterly, as the numbers of children on the Fell declined, the youth club was discontinued, although a junior table tennis club, led by John Wood, followed on for a few years. Then children were going out of the parish for their education, and organised social events for young people were reduced to the annual Christmas Party and the Summer Sports Day. The latter usually takes place on the school lot, and is organised on an ad hoc basis when the weather forecast is good.

Social Life

Cartmel Fell Societies

Apart from sporting activities (largely for male enjoyment), the main social events for both sexes in the early years of the last century would have been occasional picnics and outings in the summer, and card parties in the winter. But with the emergence of communal organisations and social groups after the first World War, the need grew for a community centre. In 1940, a piece of land between Burblethwaite Hall and Greenthorn was given to the community by the Argles family for the construction of a parish hall. A charitable trust was set up to hold the property, and fund-raising events to finance the building were held in the school. However, building costs rose nearly as fast as the building fund, and when a ready-made building in the form of the now redundant school became available in 1971, its conversion was the obvious choice.

The Trust deed of the charity specified that the committee should consist of representatives of the organisations likely to use the hall. In 1940 these were: the Parish Council, The PCC, the Women's Institute, The Mothers' Union, the Cartmel Fell Nursing Association, the Men's Club, and the Girls' Friendly Society. The Mothers' Union and the Women's Institute provided a social life for the ladies of the parish, many of whom lived on remote farms, without telephones or cars, and with little opportunity for mingling with their own sex.

17. Trick photo taken by Mr Cragghill of William Taylor and Mrs Cragghill.

18. Vicarage tea party on the Lot about 1908.
1 – Mrs Cragghill, 3 – Lizzie Taylor, 6 – Jane Taylor, 10 – Mr Cragghill.

Cartmel Fell

19. Fancy Dress party in the school, 1939.

Social Life

19. Fancy Dress party in the school, 1939.(Opposite)
Top: 1 – Ted Sharpe, 2 – Mrs Sharpe,
3 – Mrs Carruthers, 4 – Frankie Crowe,
5 – Norman Kellett, 6 – Dodge Phizacklea,
7 – Mrs Harrison, 8 – Mrs Kellett, 9 – Bill Cannon,
10 – Eileen Kellett, 11 – Mary Kellett,
13 – Margaret Inman.
Middle: 1 – Tom Mark, 2 – William Matthews,
3 – Jim Wright, 4 – Connie Parkinson,
5 – Johnnie Kellett, 6 – Geoffrey Harrison,
7 – John Taylor, 8 – Harold Ellis, 10 – Elsie Barrow,
11 – Sally Langford, 12 – Mary Ellis,
13 – Mrs Harrison, 14 – Marjorie Ellis,
15 – Bessie Sharpe, 16 – Edith Taylor, 17 – Mrs Crowe,
19 – Elizabeth Walker, 20 – Emily Walling,
21 – Edith Willan.
Front row adults: 1 – May Moffat, 2 – Ellie Haddow,
3 – Ruth Barrow 4 – Ms Ridding,
5 – Gladys Phizacklea, 6 – Lizzie Phizacklea,
7 – Mary Walker, 8 – Jessie Harrison,
9 – Elsie Matthews.
Children: 1 – Marjorie Clarke, 2 – Gwen Clarke,
3 –Eileen Wilkinson, 4 – Doris Haddow, 5 – Frances Scott,
6 – George Clarke, 7 – Ernie Shepherd,
8 – Alan Shepherd.

20. Outing to Grange – early 1920s.
2 – Mrs Thornburrow, 5 – Mrs Trotter, 9 & 10 Hilda Chapman, Mary Walker,
11 – Mrs Hudson, 12 – G. Hudson, 13 – Mrs Dickinson, 15 – B. Dickinson,
24 – Miss Flora Holyday.

Cartmel Fell Women's Institute was founded in 1928, with the vicar's wife, Mrs. Clayton, being the driving force. She became the first President with Miss Robinson the Vice-President and Mrs. Gilpin Secretary. The first general meeting was held on September 25th in the dining room of Hodge Hill, where the Misses Robinson lived. Two founder members remember walking two miles to meetings, and doing so with pleasure. The lectures were a reflection of their lives, and of benefit to them, on such topics as String Seating, Jute Rug-making, Home Nursing, Soft Toy Making, and Leatherwork. Advice was given on curing rabbit pelts, possibly for use in glove-making.

In the thirties, Mrs. Cragghill was teaching members cookery, and talks during the war reflected the conditions of the time – Cheerful Rationing, Refooting Stockings, and Knitting for Europe. In lighter moments, members enjoyed their

Cartmel Fell

21. Mothers' Union outing to Coniston, 1925.
Top: 1 – Ella Batty, 2 – Annie Batty (junior), 3 – Annie Carruthers,
4 – Becky Carruthers.
Below: 1 – Mrs Annie Batty, 2 – Edith Atkinson 3 – Mrs Clayton, 4 – Mrs A. Taylor,
5 – Elsie Pennington, 6 – Annie Taylor, 7 – Revd. George Clayton.

Rummage Sales, and some of the money raised helped to support summer trips by charabanc. There were dances in the schoolroom for good causes, and the monthly competition has caused much amusement – "Peeling a Potato Blindfolded" crops up regularly over 20 years, as does "Lighting a Candle many times with One Match". In the days of long hair "Doing one's Hair in Five Minutes without using a Mirror" must have been a severe challenge to many, but five seconds might suffice today! Another competition was to make an upholstered footstool from 2lb. syrup tins tied together. One of the entries still survives in Hawkshead, more than 50 years on.

Today, the W.I. continues to flourish, along with recently-formed Society for Scottish Country Dancing, and the Cartmel Fell and District Local History Society. Thus the old school, now the village hall, is still a focal point for social life on the Fell.

25. (Opposite page) Members of the Cartmel Fell Local History Society studying the buildings at Pattison How, June 1997. 1 – Tony Brennand,
2 – Jean Caldwell, 3 – Irene Brennand,
4 – Jennifer Forsyth, 5 – Jane Crowe,
6 – John Caldwell.

Social Life

22. W.I outing to Dalemain, 1978.
1 – Gladys Lishman,
2 – Marjorie Matthews,
3 – Peggy Ainsworth,
4 – Dorothy Ainsworth,
5 – Dorothy Grant,
6 – Ruth Smith,
7 – Jennifer Moffatt,
8 – Edna Smith.

24. Doreen Williamson, Ruth Smith and Jean Caldwell practising a new skill on a W.I. dry stone walling day near Bardsea, May 2000.

23. W.I. 70th anniversary celebration, 1998. Founder member Edie Taylor preparing to cut the cake with President Jean Caldwell and Gladys Lishman.

Politics

That very little has been said on this topic is perhaps because politics seem not to have loomed large in social life on the Fell. One suspects that conservatism with both small and large C pervaded local parishes. If farmers were tenants, they could not be seen to go against their landlords, and if they were yeomen, the status quo was better than the unknown.

It is only in the early 20th century that we come across a little light-hearted banter on political rivalries. The postman James Long, pictured in Plate 29 of Chapter 2, wrote a very long and convoluted poem about a "Tory Social" which must have been held around 1910 when Tariff Reform was a topic of political debate. Long himself was obviously a Radical, his employer being the Post Office and faceless, and he poked fun at the reasons for his friends and neighbours voting Tory. Many of the people mentioned feature elsewhere in this book, so a few lines are quoted below:

Tommy Lishman[1] fetched t'melodian, but was downhearted and folorn,
He couldn't think what tunes to play, he missed getting Tarriff Reform.
Rowly Lang[2] an Billy was ext, but sed they wadn't gang,
When Fred[3] mentioned dancing, Billy sed "Thoo knaas t'flewer's nirt sa strang".

John Fleming tew enjoyed hissel', now John's a yam-made fool,
He wad be any colour they exed him, he carts their cooals ta school.

William Taylor[4] boasts that nivver a man will torn or bring him tull,
But William torned yan day an' sed nowt ye kna, he keeps a Radical bull.

John Kellett, he turned up i'style, he's olas on the lurch,
Ye can't blame him for saying he's Tory, ye kna they'e gaan to roughcast t'church[5].

[1] The Lishmans of Bridge House were noted step-dancers, Tommy playing his melodeon.
[2] Rowland and Billy Long, pictured on the front cover.
[3] Fred Cockerton, also pictured on the front cover.
[4] See Plate 23, Chapter 5.
[5] This last line suggests that this was the time of the restoration of St. Anthony's (see Chap.3) i.e.1910/11.

This Tory Social seems to have been a memorable event, because it gave rise to another poem, – "A Song of Bliss and Woe" – which not only contains many allusions to rural life of the day, but makes fun of the lack of success of the Radicals (and of postman Long) in failing to have their candidate Bliss elected. The reference to only three or four Cartmel Fell Radicals as "poor sun-hatched loons" confirms their minority status on the political scene!

A Song of Bliss and Woe

You've heard o'Torry Social they hed I' Cartmel Fell
But there's other things as happened that they fergat ta tell.
There's Lang Net Jos frae Bryan Beck, he's reckoned gaily fly,
He buys eggs fifteen tae t'shillin' and loves yam made game pie.
He reckons nowt o'hen roosts as belangs tae t'udder folk
But yan fine day he'll happen find t'pig in t'udder poke.
There's William doun at Collin field wain't hear o' t'tariff. Why
If they put a tax on brides cakes it would mak em war ta buy.
Ye a'ken Bryan Batty' he's a gey hard workin' lad,
But t'Torries like a horse bee mak him cock his tail and gad.
There'a anudder lad ca'd Johnny, ye'll net ha far ta search,
He's a liberator proper, but he's paid for firin' t'church.
There's Jimmy Long fra Newton, tis said he is the bard
Wat wrote o't'Tory Social, if so, he's warked gey hard.
Now Jim, he being a married man, his Spring wark's done gey soon,
His wife maks t'hooals wi her wooden leg, and Jim drops t'tatties doun.
When they heeard their member wasn't Bliss, they did the best they cud,
But the ground were wet wi watter, like Spannel Beck i'flood.
They say they'll hev a social, t'll be lang afoor they try,
They'll hev ta stop i'bed because their breeches are net dry.
When they do hev t'Liberal social to set doun they willna try.
If they dinna ken this riddle, they mun ex t'Blister why.

O' Radicals i' Cartmell Fell theears happen three or fower.
Poor sun hatched loons, they'll nivver kna' wha' butters theear bread ower.

5. FAMILIES OF NOTE

The Birket Family of Cartmel Fell

There are wills, parish registers and other documents which show that the Birkets were living in Cartmel Fell as far back as 1508. Robert Byrkehed, who is named in a rental of that date, must have been born in the 1400s, and he held a tenement rated at 11d. per annum, but the property is not named. We know from their wills that the Birkets owned Birket Houses in the 17th century. This was not the present day mansion at the northern end of the parish, but was said to be a timber framed building a little way above its newer namesake. A photograph of the Tudor building was made into a postcard before the old house was demolished, but inquiries have failed to locate a copy. We also know that Hodge Hill, Kit Crag and Swallowmire were in Birket ownership from the 17th century and possibly before.

We can get a good idea of the Birket household in 1676 from the will of James, of Birket Houses, who described himself as a yeoman. This term implies ownership of the estate, but the will goes on to name other estates: Birk Field in Firbank, Rosthwaite, Rulbutts and Smithy Hill in Cartmel Fell. The two latter farms are mere ruins today.

James had three sons, Myles, James and William, and grandchildren James and Mary. Myles, being the heir, was already in possession of the messuage when the will was made, and it appears that James junior was the farmer, as he was to have all the plough and husbandry gear, a cow called Brody, a calf, a gelding and all the sheep. The youngest son William was to inherit Low House at Smithy Hill, which was a few fields away from Birket Houses down the Winster Valley; but he died soon after his father, and we learn from his will that he became a shoe-maker, or cordwainer as it was then called. His father had decreed that he should use "*the lower end of the now kitching which is now made into a shoppe as longe as he likes to stay and work there*". At this time the family were evidently farmers or tradesmen, though considerable property owners, but a century later they had become merchants, and eventually called themselves "Gentlemen" in Victorian days.

In 1679, Myles moved from Birket Houses to The Wood, which he had bought for £240. He and his children became Quakers, and he was a trustee of Height meeting, the early days of which are described in Chapter 3. At his death in 1720, Myles left goods worth £411, mostly moneys due on mortgages, bills and loans. It was apparent at the beginning of the 20th century that the fortunes of this family had continued to rise, maintaining their roles of private bankers to their immediate neighbours. When farm incomes slumped, mortgages could not be repaid and many other holdings were added to the Birket empire.

Descendants of Myles became West India merchants and had a town house in Lancaster, but they still kept a foothold at The Wood. Eventually, James Birket bequeathed The Wood to his great nephew Robert

Families of Note

Foster in 1783. It was from this branch of the family that the well-known watercolourist sprang, Miles Birket Foster.

Despite having families of five or six children, most branches of the family died out because the sons seemed unwilling to marry. William Higgin Birket of Hodge Hill, who died in 1836, had two unmarried brothers. His own children, of which there were six boys, all either died young or remained bachelors, and his youngest daughter Eleanor alone was left to carry on the family name after she married the Reverend Robert Blackburn Cockerton. The name Birket, or Higgin Birket was inserted into two of their children's names, but in later life this became duplicated when they dropped the name Cockerton. In order to inherit Birket Houses from a bachelor uncle, they reverted to the surname of Birket. This produced William Higgin Birket Higgin Birket in one instance, which takes up rather a lot of space on an envelope. (An abbreviated version of this name appears on the War Memorial seen in Plate 15 of Chapter 3).

1. Portrait of John Birket 1810–1888 who inherited Birket Houses from his brother in 1853.
[Portrait by courtesy of Robert James Cockerton]

Cartmel Fell

2. Birket Houses.

The lasting memorial to the family is the "new" Birket Houses, designed at the beginning of the 20th century by Dan Gibson, and the gardens laid out by Mawsons. It harks back to its Tudor forebear with echoes of Tudor arches and mullions, and although some of the panelling was executed in Arthur Simpson's workshops (see also Plate 10 of Chapter 6), some was said to have been taken from Hodge Hill.

3. Hodge Hill – drawing by Bertha Newcombe.

Families of Note

4. Fred, Myles and Robert Cockerton outside the Mason's Arms.

5. Local ladies, including Mrs Cockerton of The Ashes, Mrs Matthews of the Mason's Arms, and the Misses Taylor of Thorphinsty Hall, at Birket Houses around 1909. Were they providing the catering for a special occasion?

Cartmel Fell

Birkets of Birket Houses

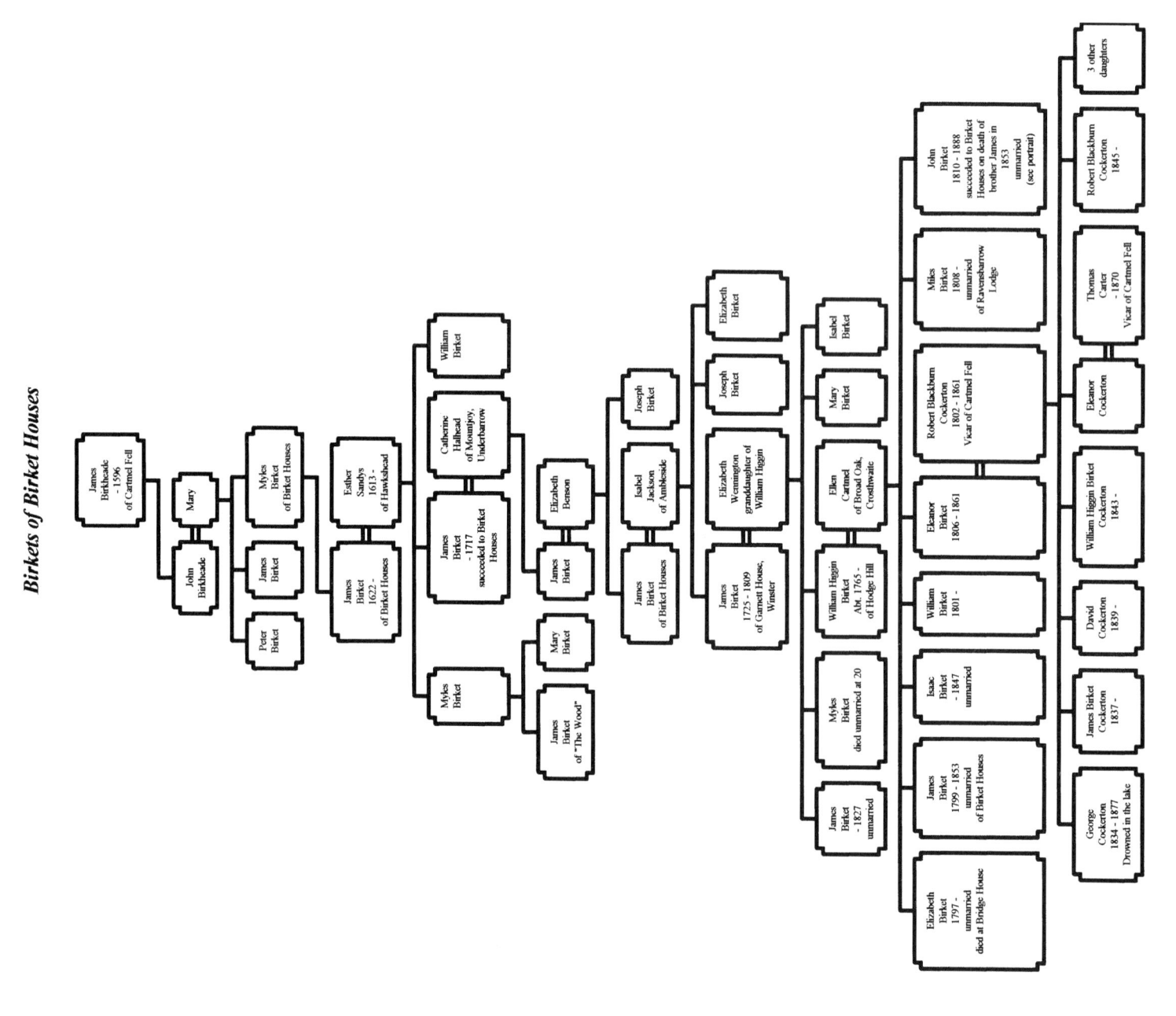

6. *A family tree of the Birkets.*

74

Families of Note

The Poole Family of Cartmel Fell

Until the mid-19th century, Ghyll Head was an industrial centre with at least two water mills served by a reservoir. The ancient Poole family had hereditary holdings at Ghyll Head and Tower Wood, but cadet branches were living at High Moor How and Prentices in the early 17th century.

The Pooles of Ghyll Head seem to have been professional men, described as lawyers or doctors. They were trustees in many capacities on the Fell, acting as such when Bryan Beck was bought by the parish to provide an income to help with the curate's salary and a fund for the upkeep of the roads.

7. Ghyll Head House

The family had its fair share of troubles, and an outbreak of smallpox in July 1797 carried off three young men, heirs to their father John, who had died in January. Many people will know the memorial tablet in Cartmel Fell church, a poignant farewell to little Betty Poole, who died in 1779, aged three years, one month and three days:

Underneath this stone a mould'ring Virgin lies,
Who was the pleasure once of human Eyes.
Her blaze of charms Virtue well approv'd,
The Gay admired, much the parents lov'd.
Transitory life, death untimely came,
Adieu, Farewell, I only leave my name.

Legend has it that the last John Poole gambled away his house and fortune in the 19th century. A descendant, R.W.Poole, who writes for the *Daily Telegraph*, recently retold the story. He mentioned that John Poole left Ghyll Head with his sole possession, a grandfather clock, on his back. Everything else had been lost in a night of gambling. Investigation has indicated that the facts are basically correct. The house was sold in the 1850s to Frederick Ward, M.A., and the Pooles had moved across Windermere to Colton. In early February of 1857, John Poole was found dead in a gravel pit on the western shore of the lake at Claife. He had died of exposure, but had been drinking heavily in Bowness the night before. He was about to row across the lake in the dark, but several people who knew the state he was in tried to restrain him, one being a local magistrate, Mr. Bellasis. Poole gave them the slip, but even so, Mr. Bellasis sent two men after him in a rowing boat. Although they had a lantern, they lost him in the dark. There was an inquest, and "Accidental Death" was recorded. Very little money was found on the body, but his widow said that this was to be expected.

About 50 years later, when Robert Matthews was decorating at Ghyll Head, he stripped off some wallpaper and found a golden guinea underneath. Could this have been Mrs. Poole's last ditch insurance?

Families of Note

The Walker Family of Bowland Bridge

The start of the Walkers' association with Bowland Bridge was in 1733 when Thomas Walker was "admitted tenant" of the hamlet by the Manorial Court of Crosthwaite and Lyth. This meant that he could pass tenancy to his descendants and it was noted in the court records that Thomas Walker the younger was admitted as Customary Tenant in 1774, his widow, Tamar Walker in 1805, and her son Thomas in 1816.

However, by 1838, this last Thomas must have purchased the hamlet because his will left "All my freehold Messuages and Tenement, Lands and Premises...situate and being at Bowland Bridge" to his nephew George of Backbarrow.

Where did the money come from? The first Thomas had married Elizabeth Bigland from Hartbarrow, a member of the wealthy Bigland family. Her father, John, who was at Barkbooth, had inherited Hartbarrow from his uncle Anthony Strickland and Elizabeth received a small bequest. Perhaps others came her way. This first Thomas was also the main beneficiary of the will of his brother George, curate of Cartmel Fell. In the 1841 census, Thomas Walker III is recorded as being "of independent means" which presumably included rents from the various properties in the hamlet. It is possible that when the new turnpike road was constructed in the second half of the eighteenth century, the Walkers might have begun selling their home brew to passing travellers. Certainly an inn was on the site in 1801 and, when George Walker of Backbarrow inherited Bowland Bridge, he became the innkeeper.

8. Thomas and Elizabeth Walker in the 1880s, parents of Richard (Plate 10).

Cartmel Fell

9. Mary Walker's mother with her second husband and grandchildren Maggie and Ted Harrison, at Collinfield.

George's eldest son, Thomas, had one son by his first marriage – another George who became a Master Mariner sailing out of Barrow. His second wife, Elizabeth Mattinson, proved to be a formidable lady who is reputed to have kept a whip behind the bar to drive out any customers who drank more than three pints of beer. Thomas became blind in later life and when he died in 1902 Bowland Bridge was left to his widow.

Their eldest son, Richard Jackson Mattinson Walker was a wagoner, with a fine team of horses, while his wife Mary ran the village shop and raised a daughter and eight sons, so for a while there were tenant landlords at The Hare & Hounds, including the Chapmans (see also Country Sports in Chapter 4).

10. Richard and Mary Walker who married at 19 and had nine children.

Families of Note

11. Arthur Parkinson, Violet's husband, outside the shop during World War II – all the signs have been removed.

Then the eldest son, Heber, took the tenancy and his daughter, Mary, (now Phizacklea) recalls life there in the 1930s. The pub was the only house in the hamlet to have cold running water in the bathroom – hot water was carried to each of the four guest rooms in spout cans. There was a flush toilet, supplied by a rain water tank on the bathroom roof, but in summer the family had to leave this for the use of the guests and return to using the outside closet.

Across the road, Mary's cousin Connie Parkinson was expected to work all hours to help her mother Violet and grandmother Mary to run the shop. While still a schoolgirl in the 1930s, her first paid job was a contract with the Post Office to maintain the telephone box. All the windows had to be polished, inside and out, the telephone disinfected, and the floor swept clean. This had to be done once a month for the sum of five shillings. Until the 1980s, the Post Office had only raised the rate to 50p!

The redoubtable Elizabeth had left only a life interest in Bowland Bridge to her son Richard and his wife Mary so long as she remained a widow. So, when Mary died, Bowland Bridge had to be sold and the proceeds divided amongst the family. The sale particulars in 1945 show that there were four lots: The Hare & Hounds Inn, together with a farm and orchard of about 16 acres; the village store and residence, let to Mrs. Parkinson at an annual rent of £10 8s.; a detached cottage (Corner Cottage) let to Mr. William Lishman (Young Billy?) at £10 8s. p.a.; and Lot 4 - "three attractive cottages" let to Miss Brown, Mrs. Gilpin and Miss Willan.

Violet Parkinson continued to run the shop until 1955, but the cousins Mary and Connie married and moved away, so the Walker connection with Bowland Bridge ended there.

Cartmel Fell

The Walker family

12. A family tree of the Bowland Bridge Walkers.

The Matthews Family

A land tax document of 1814 records that William Matthews was the owner and occupier of a homestead and orchard. The corner where he had built his house was known as "The Lound", which means a sheltered place. Today, it is a little hamlet, where the houses have changed their names several times in 200 years. The cottage first known as The Lound is probably the one which is today known as Summer Hill, after the land behind it.

The Matthews family lived in this vicinity for over a hundred years, and produced sons who were master wallers and joiners. Some lived at Bryan Beck, and some at Addyfield. In 1851, when the census was taken, William Matthews, a master waller, had many unmarried sons and daughters still living at home. Thomas and Henry were journeymen wallers, and Robert was a master carpenter who had served his apprenticeship with a firm at Grange-over-Sands. Here he also learnt to be a wheelwright and undertaker. After living for a while at The Lound, Robert bought Haycote, just east of the River Winster near Bowland Bridge. Here he added a joiner's shop, which included a saw-pit for sawing up trees and baulks of timber by hand.

After a few years Robert and his wife Alvarella moved to Strawberry Bank to take over the inn, but still continued to run the joiner's business at Haycote. Their daughter Nancy married John Hodgson, who had been an apprentice to Robert, and the young couple went to live at Haycote, but later moved to Witherslack, where John set up his own business.

Nancy's brother, Robert Leighton Matthews, then took over the joiner's shop and his brother John ran the Mason's Arms, followed by his widow and then by his daughter – another Nancy – until 1966. Older residents may remember that there was no bar until after Nancy's time-drinks were ordered and brought out from the back room, and her father used to top up the glasses from a jug.

Barwick Trustees Minute & Account Book

28th July, 1857. Ordered that William Matthews son of William Matthews of Witherslack, waller, be bound an apprentice to Robert Matthews of Cartmel Fell, joiner, for six years. The father to find clothes and a master all other things, the fee to be 12 guineas; to be paid as follows: four guineas at the end of the first three years, four guineas at the execution of the indentedure, and four guineas at the end of the term. The Apprentice to be sent to school as in former cases, ie. one month in each year during the term.

7th August 1863. Ordered that the sum of four guineas be paid to Robert Matthews as the last instalment under William Matthews indenture. Ordered that the sum of £4 be paid to William Matthews for his good behaviour during his apprenticeship and that he be presented with a Bible.

13. Indentures of William Matthews, apprenticed to his Uncle Robert.

Cartmel Fell

14. The Mason's Arms at the turn of the century.

Families of Note

15. Robert Matthews with the workforce, building Hodge Hill Barn in 1904. Robert is fifth from right, peeping between two shoulders. William Tyson Porter is in the foreground.

Cartmel Fell

16. The Joiner's Shop at Haycote in the 1920s.

Families of Note

The firm of Matthews and Son was kept busy with all manner of local work, from the rebuilding of Hodge Hill barn in 1904 (seen in Plate 15 and also in Plate 25 of Chapter 2), the Lych Gate at the Church and making farm carts and gates, sheep and pig creels for clipping and butchering, to the steady business of being the local undertakers. Funerals were still conducted with horse-drawn hearses at the beginning of the 20th century.

There was a catastrophe on one bitterly cold night in December 1925. Around midnight, the joiner's shop was found to be on fire, but because of the state of the roads, the fire engine did not arrive until 7a.m. The water froze in the hoses, but friends and neighbours did what they could, passing buckets along a human chain. This was sufficient to contain the blaze and the house was saved, but the "shop" was totally destroyed.

In 1939, Robert's son William took over the business, having been apprenticed to his father and still following closely in the footsteps of his forebears. William retired in 1982 and wrote his reminiscences of his life in the valley in a book entitled *"Made to Measure"*.

17. Robert Matthews with his son, William in about 1940.

The Taylors of Thorphinsty Hall

In 1863, John and Margaret Taylor took the tenancy of Thorphinsty Hall. Their previous home had been at Wattsfield Farm, which was then on the outskirts of Kendal, but is now engulfed by housing. A family portrait was taken in 1858 showing baby Margaret (who moved, but has been imaginatively re-touched) and her parents, father sporting a black eye which is ill-concealed. John had acquired a local reputation as a bare-knuckle boxer whilst living in Kendal, and his fame went before him to Cartmel Fell. After harvest was over, he would go to stay for a couple of weeks at The Mason's Arms where he would challenge all comers. John's family of Taylors originated in Whinfell, whilst his wife Margaret Barnes came from the adjoining parish of Selside, she being one of twelve children. Her parents, Anthony and Margaret, had eloped to Gretna Green in 1812, using a guide to take them over the mountains and thus eluding pursuit on the road.

Thorphinsty Hall was a large farm by local standards, 246 acres being recorded in the 1881 census. Except when the children were small, the Taylors provided their own man-power, having produced five boys and four girls; but eventually, three of the sons and one daughter married, though remaining for a while within walking distance of their birthplace. Anthony Taylor signed up for the Boer War, but when his ship finally arrived in South Africa, the war was over, so he returned to the family farm. One of his sisters was sorting the washing and found a letter addressed to him beginning "*My dear husband*", so Anthony had a little explaining to do. Like his grandparents, he had married secretly, and his wife was a seamstress at Witherslack Hall. Once the secret was out, the couple built one of the first prefabricated houses in the district. It came by train from Sheffield to Grange, and was clad externally in corrugated iron and internally with tongue and groove boarding.

18. John and Margaret Taylor with their first child, Margaret. 1858.

Families of Note

The bungalow was called Gateside, and Anthony established a market garden there, taking his wares to Kendal by bicycle with a huge basket on the front. A speciality, still remembered locally, were his gooseberries called Golden Droppers. He also dealt in game, as did his brothers at Thorphinsty Hall, and the account books show that "Game" could mean anything from a seagull to a hare or plovers and waterhens, but rabbits were the mainstay. The shooting rights had been granted to the tenants by their landlord, the Reverend Utthwatt, in 1868, as he thought it would be safest in their hands[1].

When John Taylor junior married Sarah, he began farming at High Tarn Green about half a mile from his parents, and part of the same estate. His brother Richard farmed at Ashes for some years in the early 1900s, but then moved to Liverpool where he became a cow-keeper with a model dairy. Grandmother Margaret Taylor was very distressed that her favourite grandson Edward was going to disappear to the far south of Lancashire, so he was allowed to stay behind at Thorphinsty Hall with his aunts and grandmother, old John Taylor having died in 1897. The railway kept the family in touch, however, with family visits or new-born calves being sent up from Liverpool to be reared in the country, and fresh eggs sent down to sell in the dairy at Otterspool.

Margaret junior, (the blurred baby in the 1850s photograph) married John Thomas Taylor of Hodge Hill, but he was not related. It was not a happy marriage, so Margaret must have been glad to be within walking distance of her family.

19. Thorphinsty Hall in the Taylors' time.

20. The newly constructed Gateside.

Cartmel Fell

21. John Taylor jnr., who farmed at High Tarn Green, with his wife Sarah.

22. Margaret Taylor senior.

Families of Note

Margaret Taylor senior died in August 1914, aged 80, but her son William had taken over the tenancy of Thorphinsty after his father's death, so things carried on in much the same way for a few more years. Eventually, William wanted a farm of his own and moved to Kirkby Lonsdale, so there was a big farm sale in April 1921. Amongst the livestock sold were about 60 sheep with mostly twin lambs at foot, six horses of varying ages, and the top price paid for a cow was £71 10s. – an enormous amount for the time. A roan bull made £57 10s.

Among the memorabilia still in family hands are account books that record household transactions. Thorphinsty Hall had a dairy herd, and the family made butter in the spring and summer. The butter was traded against groceries in a sort of barter system which other farms in the area also used, and the butter sales largely offset the grocery bill. The notebooks record the Taylors' diet in the late 19th century. Surprisingly, coffee was the main drink and very little tea was bought. Sugar, rice, flour and other dry goods feature largely, together with much boot polish, but little luxuries were in the shape of tobacco and cough sweets.

Another family heirloom is a conch shell of dramatic size. This was used to summon the menfolk from the fields if the bees swarmed, and an old photograph shows the beeboles in the south-facing wall by a barn, now demolished.

23. William Taylor, who took over the tenancy of Thorphinsty after his father died.

Cartmel Fell

24. Particulars of the farm sale.

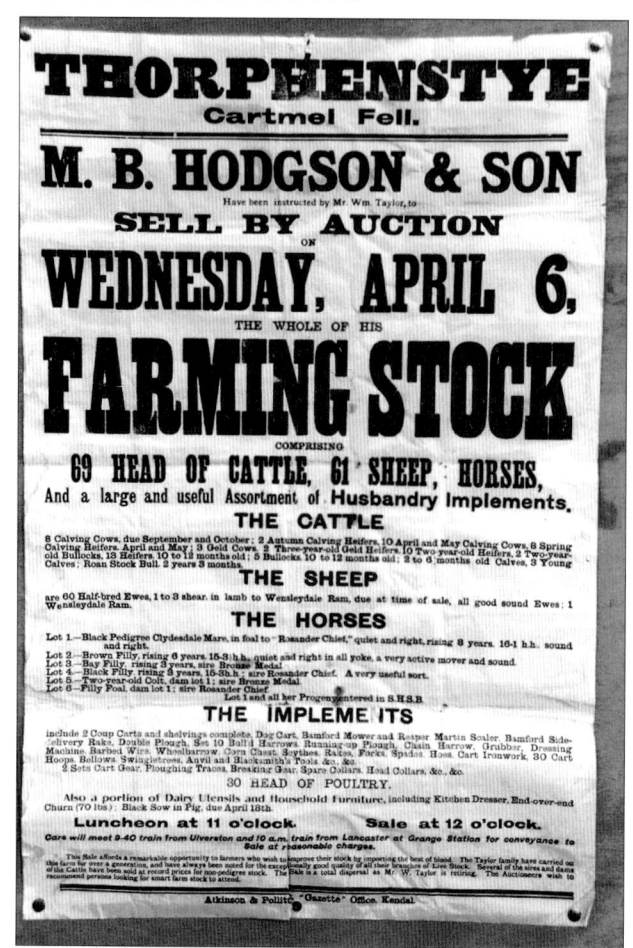

25. A good turn-out for the sale, with the women taking a back seat.

"...there was a big farm sale in April 1921. Amongst the livestock sold were about 60 sheep with mostly twin lambs at foot, six horses of varying ages, and the top price paid for a cow was £71 10s. — an enormous amount for the time. A roan bull made £57 10s."

Families of Note

The Batty Family

The Battys came to High Newton from Casterton in the first half of the 19th century, and in the 1851 census there were three generations scattered throughout the Newtons, all engaged in farming. The widowed father, William, was the founder of the Cartmel Fell dynasty, but in 1851 his household was entirely male, with three unmarried sons – John, Bryan and Thomas – all in their twenties, living at home, and a grandson James, aged seven.

Thomas was the father of Bryan Batty junior, who was newly married in 1881, aged only twenty one, but already with a son of one year, the first child of a baker's dozen. At this stage, Bryan was a general labourer, but he must have had initiative and courage, because he took the tenancy of the farm at Hare Hill in Cartmel Fell in early married life, and raised his family there. His first wife, Sarah, had a large household to cater for, and with eleven menfolk living at home, she not only fed them and made her own bread, but like most wives of the time, she made many of their clothes. Her grand-daughter Ella remembers going to visit Hare Hill and seeing her grandmother cutting out twenty two cotton shirts, all to be hand-sewn.

Five of the Batty sons were gunners in the first World War, and several were badly wounded. One had been gassed and later died from the effects of his injuries; but the others settled round about and went back to farming. William, the oldest, farmed Hodge Hill in

26. Bryan Batty of Hare Hill with his second wife.

Cartmel Fell

27. Wedding party at Hare Hill, c.1905. **Seated**: Groom – Joseph Wilson, Bride – Mary Batty. **Standing**: behind the groom – William Batty, behind the bride – Nellie Batty (later to become Nellie Matthews, mother of William Matthews).

Famous People

the early 20th century, but later took over Hare Hill from his widowed father, who had built Silver Birch for his retirement. This new house was half way up the track to Pattison How*, which Bryan then owned. Here he lived with his second wife, and together they created a garden from a piece of field. Mrs. Batty was a creative woman and designed the garden herself. She made a bank of wild flowers with the help of her step-grand-daughter Ella, planting primroses, monkey flowers, Claytonia and many others. The second Mrs. Batty died before her husband also, and he re-married a third time in old age.

Bryan III, Ella's father, was a breeder of shorthorn cattle, beginning his own farming life at Goswick Hall. He had several moves from there – first to Thwaite Moss at Rusland where his young family had the excitement of seeing an early airship; Sow How, Pattison How and then Burblethwaite Hall. Bryan became known for the quality of his cattle, but all the family were proud of their stock for which they won many prizes at local shows.

Today, the Battys have dispersed from Cartmel Fell, but their descendants are spread throughout Cumbria, some still winning prizes for the quality of their sheep and cattle.

   * Also known as Pattinson How

28. Jack and Bigland Batty, first prize winners at Cartmel Show.

Reference
1. BDB/5. Barrow RO.

6. FAMOUS PEOPLE

A few of the Fell's residents have made their mark in the wider world through their special skills in activities such as observation, design, writing and mathematics. Apart from William Pearson, they were off-comers, born and bred elsewhere, and their descendants are not among the Cartmel Fell families of today.

The Barbers of Bowland Bridge and Bryan Houses

At local auctions today, a Barber clock will be bid up in thousands rather than hundreds of pounds, whereas fifty years ago one might be had for less than ten pounds. The early clocks were inscribed "Boulan Brig", and some of these have one hand only, as seen in Plate 1. It is believed that in the 1720s Jonas Barber lived and worked at Bowland Bridge, probably in the house now called Corner Cottage.

The Barber family originated at Long Addingham near Skipton, and Jonas' uncle of the same name was a member of the Clockmakers' Guild in London. It is not known what brought the Barbers to this corner of Westmorland, and little is recorded of their early days in Bowland Bridge.

Jonas the second was born in 1688 at Skipton, and married Elizabeth Garnett in 1717. She was the daughter of Anthony Garnett of High Mill in Winster. Three of the Barber children were christened at Crosthwaite, including Jonas junior in 1720. The last, Margaret, was baptised in 1727 and later married the curate of Winster, Richard Harrison. Her sisters Elisabeth and Mary died in infancy in 1719 and 1726 respectively.

1. A Jonas Barber clock face c. 1745.

Families of Note

A smithy is recorded at Bowland Bridge in the 18th century, and it must have been fairly convenient to live close to a blacksmith who might assist with the ironwork of the clocks' interiors; but for whatever reason, the Barber family moved up the valley to Bryan Houses at Winster, bought from Margaret Atkinson in 1726. The conveyance for the sales is in Kendal Record Office. In the opinion of Cave – Brown – Cave, who wrote a book about the Barbers[1], the family probably lived in Bryan Houses Cottage, but the conveyance merely calls the estate "Bryan Houses". The sale included a dwelling house, messuage and one close called "Mousehole". What is not disputed is that the two-storied building on the other side of the road from Bryan Houses was the workshop for the clockmakers. The windows are now walled up, but there has been a fireplace, and workmen digging drains some sixty years ago found a lot of brass scrap. The workshop probably stands in Mousehole Close.

2. Corner Cottage, Bowland Bridge, with Ruth Lishman and Frances Pearson, around 1910.

Like other tradesmen of the day, Jonas took apprentices. One of these was John Philipson whose mother had died when he was a baby. John's father was struggling to make ends meet, and the baby was "on the parish", that is, getting assistance from the Overseer of the Poor of Cartmel Fell. The parish paid for much of the child's upkeep, and part of his apprenticeship fee which in 1748 was fifteen shillings[2]. Jonas Barber senior died in 1764, and John Philipson was a witness to the will which he made in 1758.

3. Sue Coyne and Jennifer Forsyth looking for Barber metal near his old workshop at Mousehole Close.

William Gibson 1720 - 1791

Little seems to be known about William Gibson's early life, except that he was born at Bolton, near Appleby in 1720, his parents dying when he was still young. He worked on a farm from childhood, receiving no formal education, but in early manhood he taught himself to read. He developed an extraordinary power of working out sums of all kinds in his head and later taught himself to write, before going on to study geometry, trigonometry, algebra and astronomy.

He moved to Hollins near Bowland Bridge in about 1740, and carried on farming whilst also continuing his studies, finally acquiring a knowledge of higher mathematics. Whilst at work on the farm, he often used a piece of chalk on the knee of his breeches, or the barn door, to work out difficult calculations. In 1745 he married Isabel German, also of Cartmel Fell, who was probably a member of the German family then living at Addyfield, which is directly above Hollins. William went by the name of "Willy o' th' Hollins" and for many years he posed and answered mathematical problems in various national and international journals. His fame spread, and he was consulted by mathematicians across Europe.

William and Isabel's first four children were born at Hollins, before the family moved to Tarn Green in the mid-1750s, where their remaining children were born. William's obituary[3] states that he lived at Tarn Green (now High Tarn Green) for about fifteen years, so it is possible that it was here that he opened a mathematics school for eight to ten gentlemen, who boarded at the farm. He also became accomplished at surveying and was appointed to act as a commissioner for the enclosure of several commons.

He lived his last years near Cartmel, continuing with his school, and died following a fall in Eggerslack Woods, near Grange, leaving a widow and ten children.

In the Cowmire box pew at St. Anthony's church is a bench with a grid pattern incised into the oak, as shown in Plate 2 in Chapter 1. If this is indeed an early type of calculator, as has been suggested[4], then maybe Willy o' th' Hollins was responsible for teaching the children long multiplication?

4. Hollins, from which Gibson derived his nom de plume.

5. High Tarn Green, about 1902, when it was farmed by John Taylor.

Cartmel Fell

William Pearson of Borderside 1780 - 1856

William Pearson's life as a farmer, naturalist and friend of the Wordworths and other notables of the 19th century is known to us because his widow published a book of his letters, articles and accounts of his travels[5].

William was born in 1780 at Yews in Crosthwaite. His father was a farmer, but in his leisure time was a great reader and belonged to a book club in Kendal, favouring medical and veterinary works. This is probably where William first gained his love of natural history and literature. He was educated at Crosthwaite and Underbarrow where he learnt, amongst other things, a version of shorthand. He taught at Winster school when he had finished his own education, and then went to teach the Dodson children at Swallowmire.

After a spell in a Kendal wine merchant's, William went to Manchester to learn banking, and his first year's savings in 1803 were £75. Nineteen years later, in 1822, he was able to buy Borderside, but initially he installed a tenant farmer. This turned out to be an unsatisfactory arrangement, because the tenant did not pay his rent. William seized the barley crop, threshed it and sold it to cover the amount due. The tenant retaliated by bringing the case to court in Appleby, but lost, after which he left the neighbourhood.

It appeared that Mr. Pearson was a confirmed bachelor. He moved into Borderside and set about improving the land, clearing the boulders and planting orchards. In 1832 he wrote:

> "My large orchard contains about 300 trees – Apple and Pear, besides a row of Plum trees …I have planted two other small orchards, with about a score of trees in each".

All the while he was writing articles on varied topics for local journals and newspapers. He campaigned for standard weights and measures, and helped to change the custom of measuring fruit by panniers of 16 quarts, to pounds and ounces. This came into force in 1832/3. Another cause he espoused was the repeal of the Game Laws. These were amended in 1831, but before that time William Pearson used his gun openly, though he had not the legal qualifications to

6. Old Borderside, William Pearson's bachelor home until he married at 61.

Famous People

7. New Borderside, built for Pearson's new wife.

do so. He also fished many of the neighbourhood becks, because he believed fish were there for everyone.

The correspondence with the Wordsworths shows that they visited each other and went walking together:

> "Next week we expect company. But after that time, my brother and I will be at perfect liberty to climb Helvellyn with you, any fine morning, when you may happen to arrive. Come by half-past 8 o'clock, and if on a Keswick coach-day, so much the better, as we could go on the coach to Dunmail Rays – Mondays, Wednesdays and Fridays, are the days on which the coach goes to Keswick" [6].

Pearson also sent them apples from his orchards and arranged supplies of potatoes, and hay and straw for their horses.

> "We are exceedingly obliged for the potatoes and apples and are, I assure you, much too selfish to desire to part with any of the latter to our friends" [7].

To everyone's surprise, at the age of 61, William Pearson decided to marry. His bride Anne Greenhow was seventeen years his junior, and they had an extended honeymoon travelling in England and Europe, advice on their routes having been given by William Wordsworth. On their return they did not live in the old Borderside, but took rented accommodation until a new house was built nearby. This was designed with Wordsworth's precepts in mind, that is with tall round chimneys on square bases. Although he was invited to visit the house in December 1849, it is doubtful if Wordsworth ever went, because he died the following April.

The Pearsons were very attached to their pets, tame fish, robins and especially a faithful old pony, Nep, who has her own gravestone down by the beck. Young Thomas Pearson, then aged 15, was living with his uncle in the new Borderside in 1851, and forty years later he was still farming there, with nine children and a wife to help him. Today, there are still Pearsons in this corner of Crosthwaite parish, but Nep lies across the River Winster in Cartmel Fell.

8. "Nep", William Pearson's beloved pony.

Famous People

The Simpsons at Gill Head

Gill Head Cottage* now half-demolished, unoccupied, and uncomfortably close to the busy A592, had been the temporary home of W.G.Collingwood**, Ruskin's biographer, until his house at Lanehead, Coniston was built in 1891; and in 1893 it was rented by Arthur Simpson. Trained as a wood carver at Gillows in Lancaster, and then in London, Arthur had returned to Kendal where he set up a workshop and travelled round the villages giving evening class tuition in carving, often walking back to Kendal afterwards[8].

At Gill Head, Arthur established a very early form of activity holidays – residential tuition in carving, interspersed with excursions to the fells. The Simpson family spent eight summers at Gill Head, returning to their house in Kendal in September each year.

The eldest boy, Hubert, attended Winster school for the summer months. Arthur himself went into his Kendal workshop three days a week and spent the other days giving instruction to the Gill Head pupils.

The sign over the door attracted visitors, including a number of clergy and the "Arts and Crafts" architects of the day, which led to commissions for churches and carved panelling in the fine houses that were being built around that time. Among them were M.H.Baillie Scott who designed Blackwell and Dan Gibson who designed Brockhole, White Craggs at Clappersgate, made alterations to Holehird and, just before he died in 1907, designed Birket Houses. In all of these, Arthur Simpson's carving can be seen.

C.F.A.Voysey was at this time designing Broad Leys and Moor Crag – both within two hundred yards of Gill Head Cottage. Their friendship led to Voysey designing a house in Kendal for Arthur Simpson.

Arthur's son, Hubert, took over the business in 1922. The period of building grand houses with carved panelling was over. Furniture and church restorations were the mainstay of the business, and Hubert was responsible for the panelling behind the altar of Cartmel Fell church, added in 1936, which can be seen in Plate13 of Chapter 3. This was made in one piece in Kendal and was too wide to go through the lych gate; the effort of getting it over the church wall gave Hubert a hernia. He was a keen photographer, and a number of the photographs in this book were taken by him.

Gill Head Cottage, meanwhile, was occupied by the Airey family, who ran a small shop selling paraffin, sweets and cigarettes. Some of their customers rowed across the lake from Cunsey.

The start of rationing in the 1939-45 war finished the business but Maud Airey stayed there until she died in 1962, after which the white painted part of the house was demolished and a modern house built behind.

---

* Renamed "Wilders Wood".
** W.G.Collingwood was a friend and mentor of the young Arthur Ransome who courted his daughter, Dora, without success, and later used her family of four children as models for the children in *Swallows and Amazons*.

Cartmel Fell

9. *The Simpson family outside Gill Head Cottage in 1894. Young Hubert is on the left with his mother and one of her friends, Arthur and Roland on the right.*

Famous People

10. Simpson carving at Birket Houses.

11. C.F.A. Voysey's architectural drawings of Moor Crag, near Gill Head.
Courtesy British Architectural Library, RIBA, London.

Cartmel Fell

Arthur Ransome at Ludderburn

Arthur Ransome bought Low Ludderburn for £550 in 1925 when he was 41 years old. He had just returned from Russia where he met his second wife, Evgenia, who had been Trotsky's secretary while he reported on the Russian revolution for the *Daily News* and the *Manchester Guardian*.

They fell in love with the house and spent most of their savings on converting the bank barn, which had previously served as a garage with doors opening onto the road, into a spacious work-room for Arthur to do his writing. Large windows, and a new floor and ceiling and a stove were added; a wooden garage was erected to house his Trojan car which he referred to as "a perambulating biscuit tin"[9]. They stayed at Great Hartbarrow while the work was in progress.

Evgenia was sometimes left alone while Arthur was sent abroad by the *Manchester Guardian* – to Egypt and China, but he preferred to stay at home and write reviews and his regular column on fishing. Their friendship with the Kelsalls at Barkbooth led to a system of communication by large wooden shapes, painted to show up against the white wall of Ludderburn and the grey wall of the Barkbooth barn, three-quarters of a mile away down the valley. Combinations of squares, triangles, circles and crosses were used in coded signals to invite each other to tea or to arrange fishing trips. The signalling system later featured in "Winter Holiday", and in 1995 was re-activated in an event organised by The Arthur Ransome Society.

12. Low Ludderburn in the early 20s, before Arthur Ransome converted the barn.

In 1929 the editor of the *Manchester Guardian* asked Ransome to go to Berlin for a year and then to become their literary editor, for the handsome salary of £1,100, but the Ransomes were settled at Ludderburn and rejected the offer. Stimulated by a visit from friends with four children (see footnote to the Simpsons above), Arthur started to write *Swallows and Amazons*. It was published in July 1930 and had excellent

13. A Trojan car entering Low Ludderburn, driven by Arthur Ransome's nephew, Arthur Lupton.

14. Amy Johnson, a regular visitor to Low Ludderburn.

reviews. This encouraged him to write the sequel, *Swallowdale* (1931), followed by *Peter Duck* (1932), *Winter Holiday* (1933) and *Coot Club* (1934).

When writing the books, he drew on his childhood memories of long holidays at Nibthwaite. In 1895, when the lake froze over, the headmaster of his Windermere school cancelled all lessons and the boys spent long days skating, taking provisions down the street on a large toboggan[10] – a happy memory which was refreshed in 1929 when the lake froze again.

This experience was used in *Winter Holiday*. His observations of charcoal burners in Tower Wood, and even the markings of the sheep in the fields around Low Ludderburn, also found their way into the books, while the Kelsall boys posed for photographs from which Ransome drew his illustrations.

In 1935 the Ransomes moved south. Perhaps Low Ludderburn, without telephone, electricity or even running water, was just a bit too isolated for one who had played chess with Lenin, and been involved in such world-shaping events in Russia. However, they never again settled for as long as 10 years in one place, their houses in the Furness and Coniston areas alternating with Suffolk and flats in London. Arthur died in November, 1967.

Low Ludderburn was bought by one Ethel Rubina Johnson, aunt of Amy Johnson the famous aviator, who visited her aunt there from time to time.

Sir John Fisher of Blakeholme Wray

John Fisher was born in Barrow-in-Furness in 1892. He left school at 17, and trained as a mining engineer in Northern Ireland. He had joined the Territorials in 1913, so was called up immediately at the outbreak of the first World War. Unlike so many infantrymen, he survived the battle of the Somme, and when he was demobilised he took over the family business, James Fisher and Sons at Barrow.

In the years between the two world wars, John Fisher's intellect and ability became widely known in shipping circles, so at the outbreak of hostilities in 1939 he was enlisted by the Ministry of War Transport as Director of the Coastal and Short Sea Division. He organised the Armada of small ships to evacuate Dunkirk, and was also one of the organisers of the D-Day landings in Normandy. He was knighted for services to shipping in 1942.

In 1947 he secretly married Maria Elsner, a Viennese opera singer who had appeared at many State Opera Houses, but she gave up her career on marrying Sir John. The couple lived at Blakeholme Wray and took great pride in their beautiful garden which ran down to the lake. They both enjoyed outdoor life, and had a shoot on the Allithwaite end of Cartmel Fell, and other activities included fly-fishing, boating and skiing.

Sir John and Lady Fisher were devoted to each other and were seldom parted. They both died at their home in 1983 when he was 91 and she was 78. Their concern to help local and national good causes, and to support charities connected with ships and seafaring, lives on through the work of foundations and trusts bearing the Fisher name.

15. Sir John and Lady Fisher, dressed in their customary black and white.

16. Interior at Blakeholme Wray – note the table made from a ship's wheel.

References

1. *Jonas Barber: Clockmaker of Winster.* B.W.Cave-Brown-Cave, Reminder Press, 1979.
2. Kendal Record Office WPR/4
3. *Obituary Notice of William Gibson*, The Gentleman's Magazine, November 1791.
4. Research by John Dench of Carlisle, 1999.
5. *Papers, Letters and Journals of William Pearson.* Published by Emily Faithfull, 1863 for private circulation.
6. Letters of Dorothy Wordsworth, 1828.
7. Letters of Dorothy Wordsworth, 1831.
8. *The Simpsons of Kendal.* Eleanor Davidson, University of Lancaster, 1978.
9. *The Life of Arthur Ransome.* Hugh Brogan, Jonathan Cape, 1984
10. *The Autobiography of Arthur Ransome*, Jonathan Cape, 1976.

7. UNUSUAL EVENTS

Royal Visits

Royalty is seldom seen on Cartmel Fell. The population is small and scattered, there is no town, no civic buildings, and no public place from which to wave. Nonetheless, because nearby stately homes can serve as suitable bases, queens and princesses have been known to tread our soil.

There was a huge flurry of excitement in the Silver Jubilee year of 1937, when Queen Mary was known to be coming on a visit, said to be a holiday, to Holker Hall. It seemed to be very much a working holiday, according to the *Westmorland Gazette*, because page after page described her visits, her tree planting and reception of many and varied gifts. One of these gifts was a tray made of bog oak by Hubert Simpson (whose skills have been noted in Chapter 6).

The Queen was taken for a drive on a beautiful day over the Gummers How road and, although the *Gazette* did not record it, she then visited Cartmel Fell Church. She was accompanied by Lord Cavendish, the Vicar Charles Last, and a retinue of ladies and gentlemen. The school children lined the path to the Church door, hoping for a wave, but Connie Thistlethwaite *(née* Parkinson) remembers that the Queen sailed past, entirely clad in royal purple, with never a sideways glance, much to the children's disappointment.

Fifteen years later, in 1952, there was a sale of items donated by Queen Mary for Church funds at Cartmel Fell. These included an Indian cloth, some cocktail mats and pink and blue lavender sticks. The sale of these items raised more than £50 (almost £1000 in today's money) for St. Anthony's, and some of the local people who bought them are seen in Plate 2.

On another occasion, Princess Margaret made a visit which was quite unannounced. The harvest festival had recently been celebrated, and Lucy Wooff had cleared the church window sills of bracken, piled it in the aisle and collected the empty jam jars. Suddenly, the Vicar appeared. "Get all this cleared

1. Queen Mary receiving a bouquet on her visit in 1937.

quickly", he said, "Princess Margaret is coming". There was no time to tidy, and Lucy was told to make herself invisible as this was supposed to be a private visit by the Princess. Lucy retreated behind the font in the bell tower, and stayed there until the royal tour was finished.

On another private visit to Holker Hall, Princess Margaret with her retinue of detectives had been visiting antique shops. They had been to Town Head and came over the fell from the lake, past Tower Wood, and down the hill to Roper Ford. It was autumn and there had been heavy rain so the River Winster was swollen. The Princess's party were in a Nissan Patrol which plunged into the water and trundled out the other side with no problems, but her detectives were in a Cortina which became well and truly stuck in the middle of the ford. It was an occasion for much royal mirth, with Princess Margaret directing operations from the little footbridge. The male members of her party joined the detectives with rolled-up trousers in the swirling flood, and managed to push the escorting vehicle to the far shore. Amazingly, it started again immediately, so the Royal Progress resumed, but with sodden nether limbs of its menfolk.

2. Purchasers of gifts donated by Queen Mary: 1,2 – Col. & Mrs Wellwood, 3 – S.P.B.Saunders, 4 – J.H.Johnson (Churchwarden), 5 – Mrs Lydall, 6 – Revd. John Sell, 7 – Mrs Saunders. [Photo courtesy of the Westmorland Gazette.]

3. Hubert Simpson's son, Oliver, on the clapper bridge at Roper Ford in the 1930s.

Cartmel Fell

Lake Winster

It is no secret that rain falls in the Lake District. Thirlmere and Haweswater have become giant reservoirs for Manchester, but even so, many rural parishes in Cumbria have no mains water. That is the case in Cartmel Fell, where all the houses, the school and the inns have private water supplies. Some are lucky enough to have a spring which never fails, but most rely on tanks fed by streams which soon dry up in hot weather or in hard frost. In a hot summer water has to be bought, and milk tankers are hired to transport it at around £40 a load.

So it was understandable that when, in the early 1960s, yet another reservoir scheme was proposed, there was much turmoil locally. The big cities needed ever more water, and Manchester looked North for an increased supply. There were schemes for small reservoirs in several Lakeland valleys. The Borrowdale valley running down from Shap summit was one of these, containing a single farm only, which says a lot about the nature of the land in the area.

Another proposition was to flood part of the Winster valley, but this was to cover the best farm land, and many historic houses. As the map shows, these included Cowmire Hall, Swallowmire, Hodge Hill and Burblethwaite Mill.

All Bowland Bridge would have been submerged, but the Mason's Arms up on Strawberry Bank would have had a lakeside aspect, as would the old houses

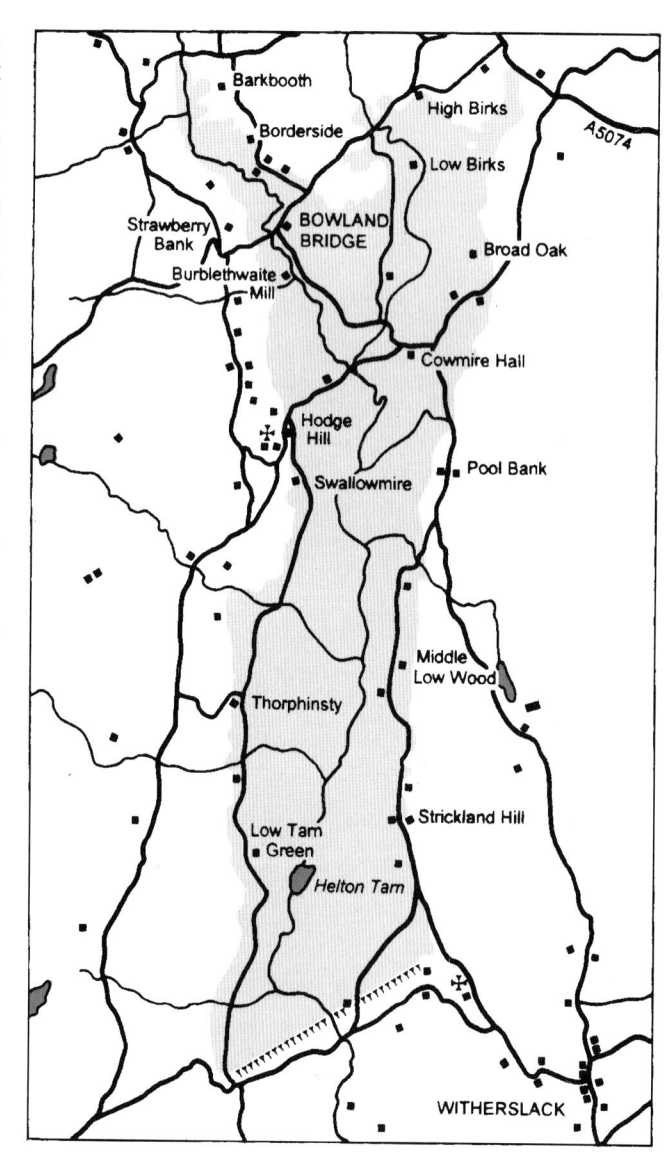

4. Map showing proposed extent of reservoir.

Plates 5 – 7 show old houses which would have been submerged.

5. *Cowmire Hall.*

Cartmel Fell

6. Hodge Hill.

at Pool Bank further down the valley towards Witherslack. The proposed dam would have been 80 feet high, and the resulting lake four and a half miles long and a mile wide.

Needless to say, there was great anxiety in the district, and the topic was aired in the local and national press at regular intervals. A photograph in the *Daily Telegraph* showed Lizzie Gilpin holding up a glass of water fetched from her own supply, which she had to carry from the spring at the side of the bridge. She carried six bucketfuls a day – three for herself and three for a neighbour. In her young days, Lizzie had been in service at Tullithwaite Hall in Underbarrow, and had kept in touch with the Willison family into her eighties. When on a visit to see Ada Handley (*née* Willison) at Heversham Hall, Lizzie related the story of a letter she had received from a relation in Nottingham. There was some indignation on Lizzie's part because her correspondent had misunderstood a newspaper article

7. Swallowmire.

Cartmel Fell

8. *Rose Cottage and Smithy Cottage, Bowland Bridge. 1960.*

Unusual Events

about the Winster Dam, and Lizzie retold the tale:

She hed written sayin' as hoo grand it wes, t' read in't paper 'at ther gaing te put Bowlan' Brig on tul t'watter. Whya Ada, she mun a bin readin' t'paper wrang side up. Ther gaing t'put t'watter ower 'top o' t'hooses, nit under t'grund.

Many protest groups were formed to thwart this and other flooding schemes, and many letters were written to the press and to MPs, frequently stressing that the National Parks should not be violated. Another proposal was for a barrage across Morecambe Bay. In the end, Manchester's demands were quelled by the weight of public opinion, and by geological evidence that the scheme was flawed. The dire predictions of impending drought by the year 2000 have not been realised; and everybody hopes that the reservoir proposal has been permanently shelved.

9. Pool Bank would have been on the eastern shore.

10. Lizzie Gilpin drawing her water.

11. Violet Parkinson and Lizzie Gilpin with glasses of their precious spring water.

Cartmel Fell

Rebuilding Bowland Bridge

The hamlet of Bowland Bridge consists of the Post Office/Shop, the inn and five other dwellings. They are all situated in the parish of Crosthwaite on the eastern side of the River Winster, which used to be the boundary between Lancashire and Westmorland.

Over the centuries, there must have been several bridges at Bowland Bridge; and a new one was paid for by Underbarrow in the 17th century. The reason for another parish paying for the construction at Bowland is not explained, but it must have been a hasty job, because only ten years later it needed repair. Possibly the bridge was renovated in Victorian times, because there are two nicely carved sandstone tablets on either side, one displaying the county and parish boundaries, and the other the name of the bridge. Three-quarters of a mile down the valley, Lobby Bridge has similar stone insets. Until a few years ago, the crisply carved letters had a pleasant appearance in pinkish sandstone, but recently they have been painted battleship grey with gloss paint.

The old pack-horse bridge at Bowland had been widened at some stage to accommodate wheeled vehicles, probably when the Turnpike road going west from Kendal began to operate in the mid-18th century; and this addition could be seen from underneath. The bridge itself has a picturesque curve to it which serves as a traffic calming measure, and is also an effective deterrent to coach parties. Some years ago, one very long coach became grounded on the hump-back and had to stay there, blocking the road and see-sawing gently until it was winched to more level ground.

Some Lancastrians have strong partisan ties to the old county boundary, and every year a small placard is implanted at the roadside west of the bridge, proclaiming that one is now entering the county of Lancashire. Someone else immediately dislodges the said placard and hurls it into the hedge.

12. View of the hamlet of Bowland Bridge in the 1960s.

Unusual Events

13 a – f. Consecutive stages in the construction of the new bridge.

14. The re-opening – John Pearson having just cut the tape.
[Photo courtesy of the Westmorland Gazette].

Towards the end of the nineteen eighties, a survey was made by the Cumbria County Council and the bridge was deemed to need strengthening. It was decided to scrap the former construction altogether and to make the road wider and level, with horizontal girders over the Winster; but the Highways Division cannot have been expecting the resulting outcry against this decision. It was clear that the bridge was held in special affection by a very wide section of the population, and not merely by the people who lived at Bowland Bridge. The reasons put forward for keeping the traditional form were not just sentimental or aesthetic, and it was probably the safety aspect which finally swung the argument in favour of retaining the hump-back. The Hare and Hounds and the Post Office face each other across the road just beyond the bridge, and a road junction here adds to the hazards. Any vehicle approaching the bridge at speed becomes airborne, so locals slow down; also the narrowness of the old structure creates caution on the part of drivers from afar.

The County Council eventually bowed to public opinion, as represented by Crosthwaite and Cartmel Fell Parish Councils; and work on rebuilding the bridge started in the New Year of 1991. Whilst excavations were taking place, a huge pile of oyster shells was uncovered by the riverside. No investigations were done at the time, so it is hard to say from which era these shells came. Large quantities of oyster shells can sometimes denote Roman occupation, but these might well have been the spoil heap from the Hare and Hounds. If so, this would have been rather unpleasant for the occupants of the neighbouring cottages, who collected their drinking water from a spring just beside the bridge.

Rebuilding work during the early months of 1991 was recorded in John Pearson's photographs; and a grand re-opening of the new bridge took place on April 21st. John was appointed "mayor" and ceremonially cut the tape to allow traffic to cross the River Winster. But first, everyone had to pay a "toll" which went towards a Multiple Sclerosis fund, as did the proceeds from all the sporting events. Janet Robinson, who lived beside the bridge, was a sufferer

Unusual Events

15. Julie Balshaw collecting the tolls.

from this disease, and she was the driving force behind this fund-raising. There were several duck races down the river, terminating at the bridge, as well as hurling the wellie, apple bobbing and many other competitive games. Refreshments of all sorts were available, Flookburgh Silver Band played all afternoon, and several generations spent their money so freely that the MS Society benefited by £2,300. And Bowland Bridge once again linked the old counties of Westmorland and Lancashire.

Cartmel Fell greets the new Millennium. Sunrise on January 1st, 2000 seen from Ravensbarrow Old Man above St. Anthony's church. Mist in the Winster Valley, with Whitbarrow and Yewbarrow beyond.

INDEX

A

Act of Toleration 3
Act of Toleration (1689) 47
Ada Handley 113
Ada Mashiter 7, 8
Adam, Bill 60
Addyfield 81, 96
Adrienne Cleasby 11
Agnes Annie Shepherd 7
Agnes Burton 9
Ainsworth, Dorothy 67
Ainsworth, Peggy 67
Airey, Henry 57
Airey, Maud 101
Alan Foster 56, 61
Alan Hewitson 13, 62
Alan Leake 57
Alan Pearson 57
Alan Shepherd 10, 65
Alec Smith 61
Alice Mallinson 10
Alison Atkinson 11
Allithwaite 106
Amy Harrison 9
Amy Johnson 105
Andrew Stelfox 12
Andrew Watson 48
Anne Greenhow 100
Anne Hewitson 13, 62
Anne Martindale 11
Annie Batty 9, 66
Annie Brockbank 9
Annie Carruthers 7, 66
Annie Metcalfe 10
Annie Taylor 17, 66
Anthony & Margaret Barnes 86
Anthony Chapman 50, 52
Anthony Clarke 12, 47
Anthony Garnett 94
Anthony Prickett 49
Anthony Strickland 77
Anthony Taylor 86
Appleby 96, 98
Arthur Lupton 105
Arthur Parkinson 79
Arthur Ransome 33, 104
Arthur Ransome Society 104
Arthur Simpson 72, 101
Ashes 87
Atkinson, Alison 11
Atkinson, Edith 66
Atkinson, Fred & Edith 5
Atkinson, Margaret 95

B

B. Dickinson 65
Backbarrow 13
Baines, Mrs. 6
Balshaw, Julie 119
Barber, Elisabeth 94
Barber, Jonas 94, 95
Barber, Jonas (jnr) 94
Barber, Margaret 94
Barber, Mary 94
Barbers of Bowland Bridge 94
Barbers of Bryan Houses 94
Barkbooth 33, 77, 104
Barker, Bill 57
Barker, Paul 12
Barnes, Anthony & Margaret 86
Barnes, Margaret 86
Barratt, Oliver 47
Barrow 13, 78
Barrow, Elsie 65
Barrow, John 54
Barrow, Ruth 65
Barrow-in-Furness 106
Batty, Annie 9, 66
Batty, Bigland 7
Batty, Bryan 91, 93
Batty, Bryan (jnr) 91
Batty, Bryan (III) 93
Batty, Ella 66, 91, 93
Batty Family 91
Batty, Jack & Bigland 93
Batty, James 91
Batty, John 91
Batty, Mary 92
Batty, Myles 7
Batty, Nellie 5, 92
Batty, Rachel 4
Batty, Sarah 91
Batty, Thomas 91
Batty, William 91, 92
Becky Carruthers 7, 66
Benjamin Fletcher 2
Bentley, Wilfred 54
Berlin 104
Bert Cleasby 60
Bert Lever 36
Bert Moon 22
Bertha Dixon 9
Bessie Sharpe 9, 65
Betty Poole 76
Bickley, Margaret 9
Bigland Batty 7
Bigland, Elizabeth 77
Bill Adam 60
Bill Barker 57
Bill Cannon 65
Bill Cox 55
Bill Moffatt 57
Billy Hodgson 60
Billy Lishman 34
Billy Taylor 7
Birch, Derek 57
Birk Field 70
Birket, James 70
Birket Houses 70, 71, 72, 101
Birket, John 71
Birket, William Higgin 71
Birkett, Emily, Alfred & Maggie 5
Bishop of Chester 2, 47
Blackwell 101
Blades, Bridie 62
Blakeholme Wray 106
Blawith 2
Bob Foulerton 60
Boer War 86
Bolton 96
Borderside 98, 100
Borrowdale 110
Bowland Bridge 36, 52, 54 77, 78, 79, 94, 96, 110, 116
Bowness 76
Bowness Church 45
Boy Scout 60
Brennand, Irene 66
Brennand, Tony 66
Bridge House 33
Bridie Blades 62
Briggs 38, 40
Briggs, Holme John 39
Briggs, Robert 39
Broad Leys 101
Broadbridge, Henry 6
Brockbank 2
Brockbank, Annie 9
Brockbank, Peggy 9
Brockbank, Thomas 2
Brockhole 101
Brown, Harry 55
Bryan Batty 91, 93
Bryan Batty III 93
Bryan Batty junior 91
Bryan Beck 33, 75, 81
Bryan Houses 95
Bryan Philipson 3
Burblethwaite Hall 40, 63, 93
Burblethwaite Hall 38
Burblethwaite Mill 19, 110
Burton, Agnes 9
Byrkehed, Robert 70

C

C.F.A.Voysey 101
Caldwell, Jean 66, 67
Caldwell, John 66
Caldwell, Sheila 27
Cannon, Bill 65
Canon Bill Greetham 47
Caroline Kidd 5
Caroline Morrison 6, 12
Carruthers, Annie 7, 66
Carruthers, Becky 7, 66
Carruthers, Florrie & Jonnie 5
Carruthers, Frances 7
Carruthers, Jack 9
Carruthers, Peggy 9
Cartmel 2, 38, 43, 45, 96
Cartmel Fell and District Local History Society 66
Cartmel Fell Nursing Assoc.63
Cartmel Priory 39, 43, 45, 46
Cartwright, Jenny 61
Cartwright, Tom 61
Casterton 91
Catholics 3
Cathy Thornbarrow 9
cattle farming 24
Cave-Brown-Cave 95
Cavendish, Lord 108
Celia Hodgson 11, 12
Chadwick, Thomas 6
Chapman, Anthony 50
Chapman, Hilda 65
Chapmans 78
Charles Last 108
Chester, Bishop of 43

China 104
"Chippy" Winder 33
Christine Rushton
   13, 14, 62
Christine Smith 62
Christine Whitton 14
Church of England 3
Clappersgate 101
Clark, Marjorie 11
Clarke, Anthony 12, 47
Clarke, David 14, 60
Clarke, George 60, 65
Clarke, Jane 14, 62
Clarke, Marjorie 65
Clarke, Peter 13, 14
Clayton, Revd. George 66
Cleasby, Adrienne 11
Cleasby, "Curly" 27, 57, 60, 61
Cleasby, David 14, 60
Cleasby, Derek 57
Cleasby, Queenie 11
Cleasby, Stephen 11, 12
Clockmakers' Guild 94
Cockerton, Fred 68, 73
Cockerton, Myles 54, 73
Cockerton, Robert 73
Cockerton, Reverend 71
Col. & Mrs Wellwood 109
Colin Wright 12
Collinfield 31
Colton 76
Coniston 52, 101
Coniston Hunt 52
Connie Parkinson 9, 36, 65, 108
Cooper, Mary 6
Coot Club 105
Corner Cottage 79, 94
Cowmire Hall 2, 38, 40, 96, 110
Cox, Bill 55
Coyne, Sue 95
Cragghill, Mary 5

Cragghill, Richard 4, 5, 9
Crosthwaite
   13, 38, 94, 98, 100, 116
Crosthwaite & Cartmel Fell
   Parish Councils 118
Crowe, Essie 7
Crowe, Florrie 7
Crowe, Frankie 65
Crowe, Gilbert 13, 14, 62
Crowe, Gladys 62
Crowe, Jane 66
Crowe, John 11, 12
Crowe, Tommy 34
Cumberland & Westmorland
   Wrestling 56
Cumbria County Council 118
Cumbria Record Office 5
Cunsey 101
"Curly" Cleasby 27, 57, 60, 61

D

Daily News 104
Daily Telegraph 76
Daisy Lishman 9
Dan Gibson 72, 101
David Clarke 14, 60
David Cleasby 14, 60
David Mason 62
Dawson Fold 3
Dent, Tommy 23
Derek Birch 57
Derek Cleasby 57
Derek Mason 62
Derek Nimmo 13
Derek Smith 12, 13, 62
Dick Harrison 9
Dickie Walker 58
Dickinson, B. 65
Dixon, Bertha 9
Dixon, Ellen 14
Dixon, Ellen & Roger 62
Dixon, Eric 14
Dixon Fox 5

Dixon, Freda 9
Dixon, Joan 12, 13, 62
Dixon, Roger 13, 14
Dodge Phizacklea 65
Dodson 98
Doreen Williamson 67
Doris Haddow 11, 65
Doris Mattinson 11
Dorothy Ainsworth 67
Dorothy Grant 61, 67
Dorothy Newton 11
Downham family 26
Downham, Jane 17
Downham, John Henry 17
Duddon valley 1
Dunkirk 106

E

Eddie Long 9
Edie Taylor 67
Edith Atkinson 66
Edith Taylor 65
Edith Willan 65
Edna Ellis 11
Edna Smith 67
Edna Wilkinson 9
Education Act (1870) 5
Education Act (1944) 11
Edward Taylor 87
Eggerslack Woods 96
Egypt 104
Eileen Kellett 9, 65
Eileen Wilkinson 65
Eleanor Higgin Birket 71
Elisabeth Barber 94
Elizabeth Bigland 77
Elizabeth Garnett 94
Elizabeth Mattinson 78
Elizabeth Walker 65
Ella Batty 66, 91, 93
Ellen & Roger Dixon 62
Ellen Dixon 14
Ellie Haddow 65
Ellis, Edna 11

Ellis, Harold 9, 65
Ellis, Marjorie 9
Ellis, Mary 9, 65
Ellison, Joan 6, 11, 12
Elsie Barrow 65
Elsie Matthews 9, 65
Elsie Pennington 66
Elsie Taylor 9
Elsner, Maria 106
Emily, Alfred & Maggie Birkett 5
Emily Walling 65
Eric Dixon 14
Ernie Shepherd 7, 8, 65
Esp Ford 26
Essie Crowe 7
Ethel Rubina Johnson 105
Evelyn Newton 11
Evgenia Ransome 104
Ewan & John Wright 11, 12

F

Fiddler, Tom 55
Firbank 70
Fisher, John 106
Fisher, Miss 9
Fleming, Hannah 9
Fleming, John 68
Fleming, John & Polly 16, 24
Fleming, Margaret 9
Fleming, Sally 9
Fletcher, Benjamin 2
Fletcher, Jenny 7
Flookburgh 2
Flookburgh Silver Band 119
Flora Holyday 65
Florrie & Jonnie Carruthers 5
Florrie Crowe 7
fodder crops 19
Forsyth, Jennifer 66, 95
Foster, Alan 56, 61
Foster, Robert 70
Foulerton, Bob 60

Fox, Dixon 5
Fran Ogilvy 60
Frances Carruthers 7
Frances Pearson 95
Frances Scott 11, 65
Frank Mills 61
Frankie Crowe 65
Frankland, Richard 47
Fred & Edith Atkinson 5
Fred Cockerton 68, 73
Fred Greenhow 57
Fred Taylor 17
Freda Dixon 9
Frederick Ward 76

G

G. Hudson 65
Game Laws 98
Garnett, Anthony 94
Garnett, Elizabeth 94
Gateside 87
Geoffrey Harrison 9, 65
George Clarke 60, 65
George Taylor 9
George Walker 77
German, Isabel 96
Ghyll Head 15, 75, 76
Ghyll Head House 15
Gibson, Dan 72, 101
Gibson, William 96
Gilbert Crowe 13, 14, 62
Gill Head 101
Gill Head Cottage 101
Gillian Holland 62
Gillows in Lancaster 101
Gilpin, Jack 9
Gilpin, Lizzie 115
Girls' Friendly Society 60, 63
Gladys Crowe 62
Gladys Kellett 9, 10
Gladys Lishman 67
Gladys Pearson 9
Gladys Phizacklea 65
Glaister, Ruth 6

Golden Droppers 87
Gordon Gregg 57
Goswick Hall 13, 54, 93
Grange 19, 86, 96
Grange-over-Sands 81
Grant, Dorothy 61, 67
Great Hartbarrow 104
Greenhow, Anne 100
Greenhow, Fred 57
Greenthorn 33, 63
Greetham, Canon Bill 47
Gregg, Gordon 57
Gretna Green 86
Gummers How 108
Gwen Clarke 65
Gwen Hoggarth 9
Gwen Rushton 60

H

Haddow, Doris 11, 65
Haddow, Ellie 65
Handley, Ada 113
Hannah Fleming 9
Hare & Hounds 36, 37, 52, 60, 78, 79, 118
Hare Hill 23, 24, 91, 93
Harold Ellis 9, 65
Harold Hodgson 53
Harold Walker 4
Harrison, Amy 9
Harrison, Dick 9
Harrison, Geoffrey 9, 65
Harrison, James 33
Harrison, Maggie 7
Harrison, Maggie & Ted 78
Harrison, Richard 94
Harrison, Ronnie 10
Harrison, Ted 7
Harry Brown 55
Harry Lancaster 9
Harry White 10
Hartbarrow 3, 47, 77
Haweswater 110
Hawkshead 66

Haycote 81
haytime 17
Hayton, Jack 9
Hayton, Olive 9, 10
Heber Walker 79
Height 19, 47, 49, 70
Henry Airey 57
Henry Broadbridge 6
Henry Hird 54
Henry Matthews 81
Herd, James 35
Heversham Hall 113
Hewitson, Alan 13, 62
Hewitson, Anne 13, 62
Higgin Birket 71
Higgin Birket, Eleanor 71
High Mill 94
High Moor How 75
High Newton 23, 37, 91
High Tarn Green 87, 96
Hilda Chapman 65
Hilda Taylor 7
Hilton Walker 7
Hird, Henry 54
Hodge Hill 1, 3, 35, 65, 70, 72, 85, 87, 91, 110
Hodgson, Billy 60
Hodgson, Celia 11, 12
Hodgson, Harold 53
Hodgson, John 81
Hodgson, Laura 60, 62
Hoggarth, Gwen 9
Holehird 101
Holker Hall 46, 108, 109
Holland, Gillian 62
Holland, Neville 57
Holland, Stuart 14
Hollins 96
Holme, James 33
Holt, Walter 57
Holyday, Flora 65
Hubert Simpson 101, 108
Hudson, Mary 11

I

Ian Nicholson 14
Inman, Margaret 65
Irene Brennand 66
Isaac Robinson 6
Isabel German 96

J

J.H.Johnson 109
Jack & Bigland Batty 93
Jack Carruthers 9
Jack Gilpin 9
Jack Hayton 9
Jackson, Martin 60
Jacky Ridding 10
James Batty 91
James Birket 70
James Fisher & Sons, Barrow 106
James Harrison 33
James Herd 35
James Holme 33
James Long 37, 68
James Smith 60, 61
Jane Clarke 14, 62
Jane Crowe 66
Jane Downham 17
Jane Taylor 63
Janet Robinson 118
Janet Whitton 13, 14, 62
Jean Caldwell 66, 67
Jean Martindale 11
Jean McGowan 6
Jennifer Forsyth 66, 95
Jennifer Moffatt 67
Jenny Cartwright 61
Jenny Fletcher 7
Jessie Harrison 65
Jim and Eileen Lupton 62
Jim Wright 57, 65
Jimmy Nicholson 17
Jo Trickett 23, 24
Joan Dixon 12, 13, 62

Joan Ellison 6, 11, 12
John & Margaret Taylor 7, 86
John & Molly Wood 37
John & Polly Fleming 16, 24
John Barrow 54
John Batty 91
John Birket 71
John Caldwell 66
John Crowe 11, 12
John Fisher 106
John Fleming 68
John Henry Downham 17
John Hodgson 81
John Kellett 68
John Kitching 60
John Mallinson 10
John Matthews 81
John Napier 2
John Pearson 118
John Philipson 95
John Poole 76
John Strickland 29
John Taylor 21, 56, 65, 87
John Taylor jnr 56, 87, 88
John Taylor senior 56
John Thomas Taylor 87
John White 6
John Wood 36, 62
Johnnie Kellett 65
Johnny Twigge 13, 14, 62
Johnson, Amy 105
Johnson, Ethel Rubina 105
Johnson, Michael 12
Jonah Walker 2
Jonas Barber 94, 95
Jonas Barber junior 94
Jopson, Mossop 14
Joseph Waring 6
Joseph Wilson 92
Julie Balshaw 119

K

Kellett, Eileen 9
Kellett, Gladys 9, 10

Kellett, John 68
Kellett, Mary 9
Kellett, Norman 9, 65
Kelsall 104, 105
Ken Park 57
Kendal 26, 40, 46, 86, 87, 98, 101
Kendal Jubilee Club 57
Kendal Record Office 49, 95
Kenneth Stone 29
Kidd, Caroline 5
Kirkby Lonsdale 89
Kit Crag 70
Kitching, John 60
Kitching, Rosalyn 60
Knipe 38, 40
Knipe, Anthony 39
Knipe, William 39
Knowles of York 45

L

Lamb How 33
Lancashire 116
Lancaster 47, 70
Lancaster, Harry 9
Lanehead 101
Langford, Sally 65
Last, Charles 108
Laura Hodgson 60, 62
Leake, Alan 57
Lenin 105
Lesley Wright 60
Leven Valley 13
Leven Valley School 13
Lever brothers 25
Lever, Bert 36
Lindale 2
Lishman, Billy 34
Lishman, Daisy 9
Lishman, Gladys 67
Lishman, Myrtle 7
Lishman, Ruth 95
Lishman, Tom 31
Lishman, Tommy 68

Lishman, William 79
Lishmans 58
Liverpool 87
Lizzie Gilpin 113, 115
Lizzie Phizacklea 65
Lizzie Taylor 63
Lobby Bridge 116
Long Addingham 94
Long, Eddie 9
Long, James 37, 68
Long, Rowland & Billy 68
Lord Cavendish 108
Louise Tongue 61
Lound, The 81
Low House 70
Low Ludderburn 104, 105
Low Wood 31
Lucy Wooff 11, 13, 108
Ludderburn 104
Lunesdale 52
Lunesdale Harriers 54
Lupton, Arthur 105
Lupton, Jim & Eileen 62
Lupton, Millie 60
Lupton, Trevor 12, 13, 60
Lych Gate 85
Lyth valley 3

M

M.H.Baillie Scott 101
"Made to Measure". 85
Maggie & Ted Harrison 78
Maggie Harrison 7
Mallinson, Alice 10
Mallinson, John 10
Manchester 98, 110
Manchester Guardian 104
Manorial Court of
  Crosthwaite & Lyth 77
Margaret Atkinson 95
Margaret Barber 94
Margaret Bickley 9
Margaret Fleming 9
Margaret Inman 65

Margaret Taylor 87, 88
Margaret Taylor snr 89
Margaret Tyson 36
Maria Elsner 106
Marjorie Clark 11
Marjorie Clarke 65
Marjorie Ellis 9, 65
Marjorie Matthews 67
Mark, Tom 65
Martin Jackson 60
Martindale, Anne 11
Martindale, Jean 11
Mary Walker 65
Mary Barber 94
Mary Batty 92
Mary Cooper 6
Mary Cragghill 5
Mary Ellis 9, 65
Mary Hudson 11
Mary Kellett 9, 65
Mary Phizacklea 79
Mary Taylor 7
Mary Walker 17, 36, 78
Maryland 49
Mashiter, Ada 7, 8
Mason, David 62
Mason, Derek 62
Mason's Arms
  37, 81, 86, 110
Matthews, Elsie 9
Matthews, Henry 81
Matthews, John 81
Matthews, Marjorie 67
Matthews, Nancy 7, 61, 81
Matthews, Nellie 9
Matthews, Robert
  76, 81, 83, 85
-Matthews, Robin 7
Matthews, Thomas 81
Matthews, William
  9, 57, 65, 81, 85
Mattinson, Doris 11
Maud Airey 101
Mawsons 72

May Moffat 65
McGowan, Jean 6
Men's Club 63
Metcalfe, Annie 10
Michael Johnson 12
Michael Smith 62
Mike Smith 60, 61
Miles Birket Foster 71
Millie Lupton 60
Mills, Frank 61
Miss Brown 79
Miss Mashiter 8, 10
Miss Robinson 65
Miss Willan 79
Misses Robinson 65
Misses Taylor 73
Moffat, May 65
Moffatt, Bill 57
Moffatt, Jennifer 67
Moon, Bert 22
Moor Crag 101
Moor How 54
Morecambe 11
Morecambe Bay 115
Morrison, Caroline 6, 12
Mossop Jopson 14
Mothers' Union 63
Mousehole 95
Mousehole Close 95
Mr & Mrs Smith 54
Mr Cragghill 63
Mr. Bellasis 76
Mr. Cragghill 5, 6
Mr. Hotblack 3
Mrs A.Taylor 66
Mrs Bentley 54
Mrs Carruthers 65
Mrs Clayton 66
Mrs Cockerton 73
Mrs Cragghill 63
Mrs Crowe 65
Mrs Dickinson 65
Mrs Harrison 65
Mrs Hudson 65

Mrs Johnson 52
Mrs Kellett 65
Mrs Lydall 109
Mrs Matthews 73
Mrs Saunders 109
Mrs Sharpe 65
Mrs Thornburrow 65
Mrs Trotter 65
Mrs. Clayton 65
Mrs. Cragghill 65
Mrs. Gilpin 65, 79
Mrs. Morrison 36
Mrs. Parkinson 36
Mrs. Poole 76
Mrs. Walker 36
Mrs.O'Flynn 15
Ms Ridding 65
MS Society 119
Myles Batty 7
Myles Cockerton 54, 73
Myles, William 2
Myrtle Lishman 7

N

Nancy Matthews 7, 61, 81
Nancy Pearson 7
Nellie Batty 92
Nellie Matthews 9
Nelson, Tom 55
Nep 100
Neville Holland 57
Newcombe, Bertha 43, 72
Newton, Dorothy 11
Newton, Evelyn 11
Newton, Lawrence 47
Newton, Pat 11, 12, 62
Newton, Tom 28
Nibthwaite 105
Nicholson, Ian 14
Nicholson, Jimmy 17
Nicholson, William 55
Nimmo, Derek 13
Norman Kellett 9, 65
Northern Ireland 106

O

O'Flynn, Patrick 12
O'Flynn, Sharon 12, 13
Ogilvy, Fran 60
Old & Young Billy 33
Olive Hayton 9, 10
Oliver Barratt 47
Oliver Simpson 109
Ossie (Tom)Twigge 62
Otterspool 87
Overseer of the Poor 95
Oxford 3

P

Palestine 24
Parish Council 63
Parish Hall 1, 30, 63
Park, Ken 57
Parkinson, Arthur 79
Parkinson, Connie
  9, 36, 65, 108
Parkinson, Violet 36, 115
Pat Newton 11, 12, 62
Patrick O'Flynn 12
Pattison How 93
Paul Barker 12
Paul Whitton 12, 13, 62
PCC 63
Pearson, Alan 57
Pearson, Frances 95
Pearson, Gladys 9
Pearson, John 118
Pearson, Nancy 7
Pearson, Thomas 100
Pearson, William 98
Pearsons 58
peat-cutting 30
Peggy Ainsworth 67
Peggy Brockbank 9
Peggy Carruthers 9
Penellum, Susan 12, 13
Pennington, Elsie 66
Penny Twigge 12, 13, 62

Penrith 35
Peter Clarke 13, 14
Peter Duck 105
Philipson, Bryan 3
Philipson, John 95
Phizacklea, Dodge 65
Phizacklea, Mary 79
pig-farming 27
Podnet Moss 61
Pool Bank 113
Poole, Betty & John 76
Poole Family 75
Porter, William Tyson 32
Post Office 79, 118
poultry 27
Prentices 75
Preston, Thomas of Holker 47
Price, Revd. Thomas 43
Price, Thomas 44, 45, 46
Prickett, Anthony 49
Princess Margaret 108, 109
Proddy, Thomas 2

Q

Quakers 3, 47, 70
Queen Anne's Bounty 1, 39
Queen Mary 108
Queenie Cleasby 11
Queen's College 3

R

R.W.Poole 76
Rachel Batty 4
Rankthorns 33
Ransome, Arthur 33, 104
Ransome, Evgenia 104
Religious Soc. of Friends 47
Rev. Robert Blackburn
   Cockerton 71
Revd John Sell 109
Revd. George Clayton 66
Revd. Thomas Price 43
Revd. William Summers 42
Reverend Utthwatt 87

Richard & Mary Walker 78
Richard Cragghill 4, 5, 9
Richard Frankland 47
Richard Harrison 94
Richard Jackson Mattinson
   Walker 78
Richard Taylor 54, 87
Richard Walker 17
Ridding, Jacky 10
River Winster
   100, 109, 116, 118
Robert Byrkehed 70
Robert Cockerton 73
Robert Foster 70
Robert Leighton Matthews 81
Robert Matthews
   76, 81, 83, 85
Robin Matthews 7
Robinson, Isaac 6
Robinson, Janet 118
Roger Dixon 13, 14
Roger Van Beevers 12
Ronnie Harrison 10
Roper Ford 109
Rosalyn Kitching 60
Rosthwaite 70
Rowland & Billy Long 68
Royal Wedding 62
Rulbutts 70
Rushton, Christine
   13, 14, 62
Rushton, Gwen 60
Ruskin 101
Rusland 93
Russia 104, 105
Ruth Barrow 65
Ruth Glaister 6
Ruth Lishman 95
Ruth Smith 61, 67

S

S.P.B.Saunders 109
Sally & Simon Twigge 62
Sally Fleming 9

Sally Langford 65
Sarah Batty 91
Sarah Taylor 87, 88
Scott, Frances 11, 65
Scottish Country Dancing 66
Seathwaite 1
Sell, Revd John 109
Selside 86
Shap 110
Sharon O'Flynn 12, 13
Sharpe, Bessie 9, 65
Sharpe, Ted 65
Sheena Cleasby 14
sheep 26
Sheffield 86
Sheila Caldwell 27
Shepherd, Agnes Annie 7
Shepherd, Alan 10, 65
Shepherd, Ernie 7, 8, 65
Sidney Walker 4
Silver Birch 93
Simon Twigge 14
Simpson, Arthur 72, 101
Simpson family 102
Simpson Ground 39
Simpson, Hubert 101
Simpson, Oliver 109
Simpsons 101
Skipton 94
Smith, Derek 12, 13
Smith, Edna 67
Smith, James 60, 61
Smith, Michael 62
Smith, Ruth 67
Smith, Sue 60
Smithy Hill 70
Smyth, Thomas 39
Society for Scottish Country
   Dancing 66
South Africa 86
Sow How 56, 93
St. Anthony 39
St. Leonard 45
St. Peter in Chains 45

Staveley 2
Stelfox, Andrew 12
Stephen Cleasby 11, 12
Stock Moss 4
Stockdale 43
Stone, Kenneth 29
Strawberry Bank
   36, 37, 81, 110
Strickland, Anthony 77
Strickland, John 29
Stuart Holland 14
Sue Coyne 95
Sue Smith 60
Summer Hill 81
Summers, Revd. William 42
Summers, William 1
Susan Penellum 12, 13
Swallowdale 105
Swallowmire 70, 98, 110

T

Tamar Walker 77
Tarn Green 96
Taylor 56
Taylor, Anthony 86
Taylor, Billy 7
Taylor brothers 20
Taylor, Edie 67
Taylor, Edith 65
Taylor, Edward 87
Taylor, Elsie 9
Taylor, Fred 17
Taylor, George 9
Taylor, Hilda 7
Taylor, John 21, 56, 65, 87
Taylor, John jnr 56, 87, 88
Taylor, John snr 56
Taylor, John & Margaret
   7, 86
Taylor, John Thomas 87
Taylor, Margaret 87, 88
Taylor, Margaret (snr) 89
Taylor, Mary 7
Taylor, Richard 54, 87

Taylor, Sarah 87, 88
Taylor, William
   17, 63, 68, 89
Taylors 26
Taylors of Thorphinsty Hall
   54, 86
Ted Harrison 7
Ted Sharpe 65
The Lound 81
The Wood 70
Thirlmere 110
Thomas and Elizabeth Walker
   77
Thomas Batty 91
Thomas Briggs 39
Thomas Brockbank 2
Thomas Chadwick 6
Thomas Matthews 81
Thomas Pearson 100
Thomas Preston of Holker 47
Thomas Price 45
Thomas Proddy 2
Thomas Walker 77
Thomas Walker III 77
Thornbarrow, Cathy 9
Thorphinsty Hall 24, 86, 87,
   89
Thwaite Moss 93
Tom Cartwright 61
Tom Fiddler 55
Tom Lishman 31
Tom Mark 65
Tom Nelson 55
Tom Newton 28
Tom Twigge 13, 14
Tommy Crowe 34
Tommy Dent 23
Tommy Lishman 68
Tongue, Louise 61
Tony Brennand 66
Tower Wood 75, 105, 109
Town Head 109
Trevor Lupton 12, 13, 60
Trickett, Jo 23, 24

Trojan car 104
Trotsky 104
Tullithwaite Hall 113
turkeys 27
Twigge, Penny 12, 62
Twigge, Simon 14
Twigge, Tom 13
Tyson, Margaret 36

U

Ulverston 10
Underbarrow 98, 113, 116
Utthwatt, Reverend 87

V

Van Beevers, Roger 12
Violet Parkinson 36, 79, 115
Virginia 49

W

W.G.Collingwood 101
Wakefield, Mary 49
Wakefields 33
Walker, Richard Jackson Mattinson 78
Walker, Dickie 58
Walker, Elizabeth 65
Walker Family 36, 77
Walker, George 77
Walker, Harold 4
Walker, Heber 79
Walker, Hilton 7
Walker, Jonah 2
Walker, Mary 17, 36, 78
Walker, Richard 17
Walker, Richard & Mary 78
Walker, Sidney 4
Walker, Tamar 77
Walker, Thomas & Eliz. 77
Walkers 36
Walling, Emily 65
Walter Holt 57
War Memorial 46, 71
Ward, Frederick 76

Waring, Joseph 6
Watson, Andrew 48
Wattsfield Farm 86
Way Beck 26
Wellwood, Col. & Mrs 109
Westmorland 116
Westmorland Gazette 5, 108
Whinfell 86
Whitbarrow 24
White Craggs 101
White, Harry 10
White, John 6
Whitton, Christine 14
Whitton, Janet 13, 62
Whitton, Paul 12, 13, 62
Wilders Wood 101
Wilfred Bentley 54
Wilkinson, Edna 9
Wilkinson, Eileen 65
Willan, Edith 65
William and Mary 47
William Batty 91, 92
William Gibson 96
William Higgin Birket 71
William Lishman 79
William Matthews 9, 57, 65, 81, 85
William Myles 2
William Nicholson 55
William Pearson 98
William Summers 1
William Taylor 17, 63, 68, 89
William Tyson Porter 32
Williamson, Doreen 67
Willison 113
Willy o' th' Hollins 96
Wilson, Jonathan 47, 49
Wilson, Joseph 92
Windermere 33, 105
Winster 94, 95, 98, 101
Winter Holiday 105
Witherslack 13, 81, 113
Witherslack Hall 86

Women's Institute 63, 65
Wonderful Walker 1
Wood, John 36
Wood, John & Molly 37
Wooff, Lucy 11, 13, 108
Wordsworth 1, 98, 100
Wrestling 56
Wright, Colin 12
Wright, Ewan & John 11
Wright, Ewan and John 12
Wright, Jim 57, 65
Wright, Lesley 60

Y

Yews 98
Young Billy 33

Suggested Reading

William Rollinson, *The Lake District, Life and Traditions*. Weidenfeld and Nicholson.

Susan Denyer, *Traditional Buildings and Life in the Lake District*. The National Trust, Victor Gollancz. 1991.

Letters, Papers and Journals of William Pearson, edited by his widow. The Victoria Press Hanover Square, London . 1863.

J. D. Marshall, M.Davies-Shiel. *Industrial Archaeology of the Lake Counties*. Michael Moon, Beckermet, 1969 and 1977.

Michael Newton, *Six of The Best*. M. Newton, Edmondbyers, 2000

James Stockdale. *Annals of Cartmel*. William Kitchin, Market Street, Ulverston, 1872.

J. C. Dickinson. *The Land of Cartmel, a History*. Titus Wilson, Highgate, Kendal, 1980.

Lightwood Cottage   Lightwood   The Mason's Arms   Goswick Hall   Addyfield   The Lound

Burblethwaite Hall   Burblethwaite Mill   Broad Oak   Bowland Bridge   Hollins